BUSH REFUSES TO SURRENDER

N. Haridas

Publications

KALPAZ PUBLICATIONS
DELHI - 110 052

Bush Refuses To Surrender

Rs. 540

ISBN : 81-7835-353-9

Published in 2005 in India by
Kalpaz Publication,
C-30, Satyawati Nagar,
Delhi-110 052
Email : kalpaz@hotmail.com

Lasertype Setting by: Tact Computer Graphics, Delhi
Printed at: Mehra Offset Press, Delhi

To

My late brother

N. Gadadharan.

Author's Foreward

This book is written in the run up to the American President Election of November, 2004. President George W. Bush, fighting re-election on the anti-terrorism platform, wants to justify the counter-terrorism war he planned, programmed and waged as his unusual response to the September/11 attack on Twin Towers. There is growing criticism that this response is unequal to the crime, and therefore unfair and unjust. But the author looks through a different angle and pleads that the Bush reaction deserves a fair judgement by people and world democracies.

The world calls American president the most powerful man on earth. If his power is measured in the power to destroy, he is truly the mightiest. But as the head of a democracy his power is not absolute and authoritarian. President is not a dictator to order anything to destroy everything. As ruler, he is governed by law and the Constitution and also disciplined by precedents, the first principles of democracy and the vagaries of public opinion. He obeys the orders of courts, the injunctions of judicial review, the admonitions of congressional enquiries, and ultimately suffers the threats of impeachment and removal, and inevitable prosecution. In the course of more than two hundred years, many democratic and antidemocratic forces were invented and unleashed in the United States, and they hunt the president with unquenching thirst. These are the press, the TV, the investigative journalist, congressional enquires, the Independent Counsel, Special Prosecutors, betrayers and informers infiltrating government-machinery, the courts armed with the shock and surprise of its new jurisprudence, the terrorists, the trauma of re-election and the mysteries that lay siege on him. In this hostile world, presidents live, work and administer the country and decide the destiny of nations. Presidency is a complex job, and many incumbents, getting alarmed of this house of horrors, run into misadventures. But a real ruler takes control and lead. The author makes the plea that George W Bush is a president in control, means what he says and is a great leader of American democracy.

To another President, September/11 would have been simply a crime of multiple murder, the kind of which takes place anywhere there are deadly criminals. But Bush takes it differently and declares that terrorism is to be fought at the highest level of government as war, and the terrorist is to be defeated and liquidated before he establishes his unbeatable kingdom, threatening world peace. To him the war against terror shall be the top priority, because the terrorist organises, works propagates and battles almost invisible and the general society is always at his mercy. The terrorist does only bad things and perpetuates his violations of peace.

The author searches through the American political system, the Constitution, the courts, the Congress, the press, the investigative journalist and the presidency. He pleads that George W. Bush, by his courage, firmness, audacity and vision is one of the extraordinary leaders in democracy's history. He is reinventing and reassuring the role of that country as world police-man. To world democracy, he promises and guarantees peace. To punish the terrorists of September/11, he invaded Afghanistan and Iraq, and the terror-machinery there are all dismantled one by one. Some say he over-reacted through military invasions, but in truth he has assembled and equipped an international machine to fight terror, and the impact of his diplomatic offensive on anti–terrorism has been very decisive. But the ultimate test of all these questions, so far as an American President is concerned, is the verdict of American people, and one such verdict comes in November 2004. But that verdict may differ from the verdict of a learned professor, the scholarly historian, and the partisan politician. Then I leave my conclusions to the verdict of readers.

Thiruvananthapuram **N. Haridas**
15-09-2004.

Acknowledgements

This book is casually planned and written. I discussed the subject of this book with academic friends and they said the theme is some-what unusual, but they encouraged me to do it. Prof. S. Narayan, Thiruvananthapuram made a critical overview of the subject and made suggestions, corrections and modifications. Also he went through the entire draft to make it error-free, smooth and outlook-oriented. My daughter H. Prabha Lekshmi and her husband Udayabhanu Sreedharan sat with me many long nights in drafting and redrafting chapters, which actually was a race against time.

On several questions, I could not or did not consult academicians or verify with experts, because this has been a job done in speed, and a work in haste usually takes its toll of imperfections and errors, than when written slowly and methodically. But in spite of possible imperfections in presentation and debate, the central theme of the book is a carefully considered one, as far as the author is concerned.

The typing work has been done by Mr. P. Sadanandan Nair and M. Santhosh Kumar. Though a strange subject to their job-practice, they very quickly readjusted their skills and carried out the work with the speed, deserving the project. The final DTP has been taken by Mr. Prasad and Ms. Asa Prasad who had to work overtime to finish it.

The publicatioin of the book has been entrusted to the reputed publishers M/s. Gyan Book Pvt. Ltd. New Delhi, who did the printing work in their high tradition in promised time, and released it to the public. My sincere thanks to them, especially to Mr. B.P. Garg, Mr. Amit Garg and members of their staff.

To assist me always is Mr. Appu, Naluthattuvila, my boyhood companion and helper all along.

I record my sincere thanks to them all-companions, staff and friends, associated with the work. To them I offer my best wishes also.

Thiruvananthapuram **N. Haridas**
15-09-2004.

1
Thinking Dangerously

George W. Bush launched America into Afghan–Iraq Wars 2003. He went to war, defying the criticism of opponents, that he jumps into fray too readily to be called a reckless arms racer endangering our planet. When Bush Sr. was president in 1988-92, he waged the first Gulf War, and reconquered and restored Kuwait to its original owners. But the American people believe that the war ended in the surrender of the United States, and victory of Saddam, and this is a puzzle still haunting military and political logic. True, it was a surrender delivered by American magnanimity, but this magnanimity argument the American voter was not ready to accept at the hustings. They were convinced otherwise that America was defeated in the war–a war that ended in a spectacular show of American power and armed superiority. The large and restive Iraqi population, who eagerly awaited liberation, and placed all hopes in the ultimate American triumph and the inevitable overthrow of Saddam, stood betrayed. As if this betrayal is not enough, very cruelly they were fed into the voracious guillotine of the tyrant, to be butchered as traitors. The liberation war was great success, but the liberated were reduced into martyrs. A historic example is the defence of Warsaw in 1944 and the Soviet betrayal. This American somersault in Iraq was a blow to her credibility and promise, and this damage could not be repaired. This is a blot on America as a diplomatic blunder. The restored Saddam never reformed his ways, and continued his inhuman social engineering cruelties with increasing dastardliness and blood-thirst. The world is wondering that this American capitulation in Iraq was as uncalled for as unnecessary. This, the Vietnam syndrome–the nadir of American defeatism coming to dominate American war behaviour. The captains of the first Gulf War at last reached an uncalled for worry, and feared any American victory as unmanageably undesirable in the complexity of world affairs. Wrongly, they premised that complete victory in Iraq was against the United Nations resolution, which supplied the basic authority to US. But in fighting and winning the first Gulf war and turning it into an open tragedy, George Bush Sr. showed extraordinary courage for defeatism, then engulfing the American political creed. For the fault of losing a war that was really won in the battlefield by American soldiers, Bush Sr. was defeated in the battle of ballots by American voters in 1991-November.

No incumbent president loses in America, unless it is a very dismal show. Post-war America has produced many such weak figures, and into the ranks of Ford and Carter, we have to enrol George Bush Sr. also. When the American army was storming the gates of Baghdad, Bush Sr., Collin Powell etc started thinking of the laws of the United Nations, and wholly missed their thought on Saddam–the killer, whom the people wanted to overthrow. Powell-the general was contending that the United Nations resolution authorises only the expulsion of Iraqi forces from Kuwait, and America had no authority to do anything further, much less to conquer Iraq. Even the hot pursuit theory of chasing the enemy until he is disabled and destroyed, has been ignored and the awful consequences we see. The offender went scot-free after committing offences against humanity. The inevitable military logic is that until the invader is disabled and punished, the war does not end, and that basic rule of military logic also has been overlooked. However, the world and the people of America will not buy this defeatist argument of Bush Sr. Resentment was everywhere and they declared that Bush Sr. betrayed America, and rejecting the Bush-Powell excuses on the laws of United Nations, they defeated the leader who surrendered. Bush Sr. suffered two defeats–one in Iraq and the other in his own home-turf.

The Clinton White House was vigorous but he never made any achievement like fighting battles and winning wars. His main policy failure was his softness towards China and his neglect of her growing military threat in Asia. In maintaining the military balance in East Asia, Clinton had no plan at all. During his reign, even North Korea attempted to acquire a nuclear bomb, but he took no preventive steps.Occasional missile and bomb attacks were made against Saddam, but most of these weapons missed targets. George W Bush ridicules that America cannot afford to fire a million-dollar missile against a five-dollar tent in Afghanistan. The Clinton reign was a favourable time for India and he made many moves to normalise relations even in the midst of the scandals engulfing him. The Clinton steps were really positive regarding India and a new era of friendship emerged between these estranged democracies. But unfortunately his administration has been paralysed by sex scandals, and the President was involved, especially in the second term, more in the defence of his person than in the defence of his country. Charges galore came to the open that the president is a shameless philanderer and there came many female beauties in different sorties to bombard Clinton on his sex-escapades. The Congress was again in sensational business, and the talk-show in the Capitol has grown into impeachment of the Chief Magistrate. Assisted by the Independent Counsel-Starr, who is the run way prosecutor also, impeachment took a heavy toll of Clinton administration, and these were peaceful intervals for terrorists to plan, mobilise, and target.

Bush Sr. and Clinton never took any active interest in formulating an effective policy and strategy in counter-terrorism, and until September/11, 2001, these intelligence concerns lay buried without any responsible look. The congressional hearings and the September/11 Commission speak sadly on official and presidential apathy in the pre–September/11 days. America wakes up only to the thunderous cry of September/11. There was no coordination between intelligence agencies, and the powerful CIA and the FBI had their secrecies under lock and key without disclosure. The September/11 Commission comes down heavily on the lack of co-ordination between these top intelligence agencies of the country, and there were no counter measures discussed and planned. The CIA chief-Tenet speaks out that until September/11, there was no clear direction and authorisation from the White House on any counter terror measures to take, like assassinating terror-chiefs like Bin Laden, Mullah Omar etc. He explains also that even the best information availed and co-ordinated would never have given a clear picture of the modus operandi of September/11, and so any disclosure, dissemination and co-ordination would not have prevented that tragedy. The terrorist ideas are updated every moment and they make it most confidential. How a thief is changing his skills and tactics once he is caught, may give us a lesson in second-guessing the future strategies of a terrorist. On human conduct, is it reasonable to say that all thefts could have been prevented if there was dire diligence on the part of police and the house owners? Some thefts could have been prevented but not all. September/11 has happened and there is no undoing it.

The Clinton legacy was not setting safe standards to be followed on anti-terror measures. If the high office was tarnished by the porno-literature of Starr, Bush Jr. wanted to make a contrary history of clean presidency. So, even after an almost full term in office, George W. Bush does not produce sex scandals, and so the media and the Congress may be sorry that they fail to seize that weapon to inflict a fatal blow on the president. Saved of this distraction, the President can now attend to his duties as world police man, a job often renounced and disclaimed by presidents, only in political humility. Saddam had been the detractor, and the electoral undoer of Bush Sr. who in the moment of triumph wanted to capitulate. Perhaps Collin Powell–the general, advocated this course in preference to a full victory, as he was more concerned of the opinion of political moralists and the laws of the United Nations Resolution. Saddam was beaten in the battle, but quite surprisingly was allowed to retain his throne and this with terrible consequences to the free-world. The large Shiite majority, who believed and pinned all hopes on America, and rose in revolt, were betrayed and the revolters were captured by the Saddam forces and slaughtered in thousands. Tens of thousands were incarcerated in gulags. A war, which came to full military victory without any battle fatigue to the United States, now stands changed into a political tragedy by her leaders. American people felt humbled, and they decreed that their country stands defeated in the First Gulf War, and that this humiliation was brought home by American political illogic and ineptness. A sitting President-the most famous man on earth on the Election Day–is failing in re-election. George Bush Sr. chose the capitulative way and joined the ranks of American apologists, and thereby seriously offending the American pride. Gerald Ford made the disastrous retreat from Vietnam, and Carter who surrendered before the Iranian terrorists was ready even to disown western Europe. But Russia did not make such an outrageous demand, and Western Europe escaped a Russian take over. Victory is a thing, which the people of an isolationist America, also wants to have, as the American common person is not yet a defeatist.

Bush Jr, unlike his father, is criticised by his political opponents that his days in the White House are dangerous days for America. He is indicted, for the rash war in Afghanistan and Iraq, exposing United States to greater dangers. But George W. Bush set out for the re-conquest of Iraq–the main enemy. Like, the First Gulf War, the battle is over within days and Saddam has been captured after a long search. Now power has been transferred to an Interim Council composed of Iraqis alone, but the war with terrorists continues. But there is a fullthroated media assault against a 'reckless President' in progress, and they say that George W. Bush had no definite roadmap for the takeover of Iraq and conduct orderly governance. Also they say that Weapons of Mass Destruction (WMD) or not, the President was determined to overthrow Saddam. They allege, he had the motive to avenge the attempted assassination of his father by the Saddam henchmen in Kuwait in 1993. Every loving son will desire to avenge his father's attempted assassination but Bush made no public vow to punish Saddam. May be he wished for an Iraqi provocation only as a tactical step to justify a predetermined cause. Right from 1997, no weapon of mass destruction has been searched out from Iraqi silos. Many times it was only grudging permission granted to the United Nations team and many times inspectors were not allowed. When Saddam banned the inspections, the suspicions soared. After the First Gulf War, inspectors could find out WMD and these contrabands were destroyed. However, immediately before the Second Gulf War, the inspections to dig out WMD were failed expeditions, as no trace of WMD was detected. Perhaps this cause on WMD failed the Coalition. Another anxiety of the UN team was the acquisition of nuclear capability by Saddam. True, he had built a nuclear reactor long ago, but before going critical, it was destroyed in Israeli bombing. Most fearing a Saddam bomb is the Jewish State of Israel. Anyhow, there is no evidence that there are contemporary stockpiles of WMD in Iraq. However, Saddam was bluffing all along that he is in possession of huge quantities of arms, and he commands a big standing army and armour capable of defeating the power of the United States. Taking lessons from the Second World War, bluffing had been an important factor in war propaganda. In the Second World War, the French and the British were often carried away by Goebellean bluffs and these countries failed to call the bluff. Bluffs were not the monopoly of the Germans. Such bluffs made a greater impact on Hitler also, who, believing the exaggerated war resources falsely claimed as commanded by Churchill, put off the invasion of Great Britain indefinitely. So when Saddam is bluffing, even the American President cannot be uncautious. Not impossible that he has an underground atomic plant and a crude bomb and the enemy (US) will actually be running into a disaster by entering Iraq in over-confidence. Even just before the war, United Nations Inspectors were despatched to Iraq and they went wherever they wanted, but to find nothing as WMD. But can we conclude that all weapon secrets have been probed and unearthed by the UN team? There can never be such a guarantee. There can be secret cellars or underground storages or secret arsenals on borders. Suppose America, believing the findings of the United Nations Inspectors, hurriedly despatched its troops to attack Iraq, but there came a WMD attack with mass casualties–what will be the reaction of the media, the Congress and the people of the United States? They will cry for the blood of the President who will be accused of making a leap into the dark and courting disaster. If there was a nuclear bomb in the hands of Saddam, may be borrowed or bought from a roguish North Korea, the Congress will immediately impeach George W. Bush, as a foolish adventurist. When no weapons are detected by the UN team, Saddam can still claim that he has a huge armoury that can wreak havoc on the enemy, and such claims can be dismissed only at great risk. Take note that even in the long and diligent searches, the United Nations team never stumbled on the hiding place of Saddam, and there can be any number of secret storages and silos which cannot be discovered without informers. Now the media is on rampage against the President for not discovering any WMD. But before the war started, was the media able to assert that there was no WMD in Iraq, and they know it finally? Now as no WMD is found out, they come accusing, that the war was fought without a true cause. If a stock-pile of WMD is found out even tomorrow, the whole media will go into hiding, only to eat their own words. This is like saying that in the last days World War II, Hitler had been unpossessed of weapons, and therefore the Second World War was unnecessary. Can a soldier walk a minefield trusting the words of a ballistic expert that the mines are all removed or neutralised? The same Saddam had waged a ten-year war with Iran, and caused the death of more than a million people in battles, and that declares the magnitude of the tragedy. In that war, he killed thousands of political opponents and massacred thousands by poison gas. How such a ghastly criminal be purged of his crimes! Luckily, there was found no WMD in 2003, but will this non-finding raise him into a new apostle? At the time of defeat, all tyrants are unarmed being disarmed. Has the media gone so rash as white-washing his crimes against humanity!

2
Versailles Treaty And American Isolationism

The fight between the Congress and the presidency is a growing as well as accelerating conflict in American constitutional set-up. There are vehement queries raised that the American Congress has deliberately sabotaged the Versailles Treaty only on petty reasons. Historians argue that President Wilson failed to consult some wire-pulling Congressmen before going to Paris, and their vanity stood offended when the Versailles Conference was making worldwide news and repercussions. The all-powerful treaty-ratifier had been ignored, and that hurt-jealousy led to the historic as well as suicidal rejection of the treaty in the senate. Political leaders and historians contend that had there been American ratification of the treaty, America would have been an active intervener in European affairs and this intervention would have contained Hitler's military adventures, saving Europe and the world of the agonies of a 6-year long blood-bath. Hitler was never interrupted by the United States. America having a sizable German population, the Fuhrer believed that under their influence and the continuing isolation, the huge American military-industrial complex would not be available for Europe, especially to Britain and France. But once starting the war, Hitler could not stop it, nor so suddenly restructure his strategy to enthuse the Americans. May be true, if America had-declared earlier her intention to intervene on the opposite side of Hitler, perhaps there would have been no Second World War. But war changes course often midway. When Hitler started the war, Japan, Italy and Russia were on his side. But after two years, Japan was fighting a separate war with the United States, and Russia switched sides and went over to the Allies, and the balance of power of the world went radically altered and the initial equations collapsed. The failure of the Axis was due to the failure of Germany and Japan to co-ordinate their strategy in the beginning stages. Political as well as military strategists point out that if Germany and Japan had jointly invaded Russia in 1941, the latter would have collapsed soon, under the two-pronged attack from—east and west. Also if Japan had not bombed Pearl Harbour, the American entry into the war would have been remoter, and the Japanese occupation of the East Asia Co-Prosperity Sphere would have been of longer duration. But the Axis, flushed with the lightning victories they got in Poland and France, tried to swallow too much in too little time, and this over-confidence and over-exertion led Hitler to 'Barbarossa' which totally eclipsed the Axis victory by the entry of general winter in battles. Anyhow, a long war meant only Axis defeat, as for the Axis everything depended on a lightning conclusion of the war. Germany and Japan did not possess long-term resources. True, these are the ifs of war and history and the historic ifs, if America acted one way than the other. Now there is a change. When America fails in her world roles, George W. Bush attempts a come back, as the new hit-man of that superpower.

America, especially pre-war America did not think of pulling out of military clashes midway, out of fear and public opinion, and this decision to insist for full victory saved the honour of America in the First and

Second World Wars. These wars were fought not entirely to defend American interests, territory and honour in the customary sense. These military labours were on human and humanitarian considerations to begin with. Once entering the war, the war itself makes its own critical demands, and every country tries its best to feed the war-machine, in preference to all other needs. People go to war to fight a full war and reach full-victory or full-defeat, and that is the meaning and logic of war. As Clauswitz said, war is only an extention of political activity. In the irrevocable march of arms, a country lands in defeat only after waging a full war, expending all possible resources. It is only in the post World War II years that America is thinking of limited wars, resulting in unlimited defeats for that country and proteges, and this dishonourable game was played in Korea, Vietnam and Iraq also. Now limited wars are the American way of life. The biggest American debacle in the 20th century had been the loss of China to Communism, and this loss was caused by a combination of defeatism and isolationism. Many people still believe that if Tom Dewey–the intrepid anti-Communist had won his presidential race against Truman in 1948, he would have saved China from falling to Communism. Truman was feeling guilty of the massacres at Hiroshima and Nagasaki and he would not use the atom bomb again. The world was hoping a massive win for Dewey, but Truman had an upset win. With the battle fatigue of World War II, he will not be adventurous again. A direct intervention by U.S. militarily alone would have saved Chiang Kai Shek and prevented the birth of Communist China as a threat to the Free World, Asia and the Far East. Only General Mc Arthur pleaded for such a course, for an all out war. But the post war policy of America, which is carrot and stick in Western Europe and in the Mediterranean, was effective in checking the rise of Communism, through proxy defences, and these defences were executed in a two pronged strategy–economic and military. But the prediction of Mc Arthur came true very soon. America had to pay a heavy price for its failure to intervene decisively in the Chinese Civil War, which could have accomplished at least a partition of China between Chiang and Mao Tse Tung. Thereafter Chinese expansion was unstoppable in Asia and the Far East, which was aided and speeded up by the demilitarisation Japan. The Japanese neutrality continues even after fifty five years, and in that country peace is constitutionalised. Red China, who could exploit the best opportunity of American neglect and apathy in Asia, was spreading its tentacles far and wide. It ran so many wars in the east, in spite of more than thirty five million Chinese dying in the famines of the fifties and sixties. These wars are–the Indo-China War of 1949-54, the Vietnam War of 1962-75, the Guerilla Wars in Burma, the conquest of Tibet, the border conquest of India and annexation of Aksaichin and claiming large tracts of other Indian territory; the border war with Russia, the claim on Spartleys and other islands, the sabre rattling against Taiwan, and so on. In all these wars, the Chinese got success because of an ambivalent American strategy of stopping the war midway, mainly due to domestic and congressional criticism. In due course, China had made it her permanent international strategy to raise territorial claims on neighbours, and these aggressive claims, brought rich dividends for her. In a compromise, China makes only a territorial gain and not a loss, and this turns out truly into military annexation. These gains have made her more and more aggressive and chauvinistic, and the aggressions in the fifties and sixties continued. Soviet Union did not bother to stop her. In the mean while,

China went nuclear, but after nuclearisation there is no instance of that country making any direct threat of nuclear blackmail; but it is fait-accompli for its neighbours that China is nuclear-armed, and so its gains of aggression once wrongly accomplished, cannot be retaken by them. And India is the main victim of Chinese aggression having lost 30000 Sq. Kms, but in those days the Indian Prime Minister Nehru, was an innocent votary of Chinese expansion, he having failed to distinguish between revolution and imperialism. Surprising that, this credulous man created the most favourable situation to cover up Chinese misdeeds under the cover of revolution. The pro-western, pro-US, Pakistan, to satisfy her malice towards India, surrendered part of Kashmir to China, and established the most favourable nation-state relationship with that country. But Pakistan continues pro-western. No surprise, they entered into devastating nuclear deals also. China was encouraged by Indian ineptitude, American neglect and Japanese neo-pacifism. Pitiable that India never fore-saw these dangerous consequences, as her leaders were pro-China idealists, encouraged by communist ideology. Anyhow, this ideological shell was exploded in 1962, when Chinese warlords came in the open for a naked invasion of India. Nehru had been warned by many, but he was determined to continue credulous enough not to expect an attack from his panchasheel ally.

The loss of China to communism in 1949 was mainly due to dilly-dillying by a weak American State Department, under an irresolute Secretary of State–Dean Acheson–who was unashamed enough to blankly convince himself of the invincibility of a Communist China. Recent experiences say that democracy is a poor fighter of her rights, as she goes to war only when pushed back to the wall. Unfortunate that in the war councils, only cowards dominate in democracies. Democracy forgets that offence is the best form of defence. If compelled to act in battle, there comes media criticism that the war is as unnecessary as uncalled for, and therefore the President or Prime Minister who opted for war shall be as bad as a war criminal. But later the same country will pay a high price for this criticism by suffering fatal military reverses. Today the most powerful military power on earth is a democracy, with rare imperial pretensions, but that democracy is placed in shackles by the media and the Congress who are jealous of the presidential powers. These two agencies abet the militancy of dictators, cannibals and genocidalist's but always failing to admit it. The American media and the Congress pursue activist jealousy towards the executive power of the Union–the presidency - a stand historically anti-state. On a closer examination, it becomes evident that the media has played a crucial role in forcing an American surrender in Korea, and most absolutely in Vietnam, and in other parts of Indo-China. To force a Vietnam collapse and humiliation the American media unleashed the demon of Watergate, and that demon preached a withdrawal that consumed millions of martyrs in the land and seas of Vietnam. What followed the American withdrawal was an unimaginable human tragedy of appalling dimensions, and this debacle stares at the growing defeatism in America. The media, instead of supporting a war to defend the freedom of South Vietnamese, were acting treasonably to oppose it, and this helped the North Vietnamese marauders to accomplish a conquest as comfortable as knife cutting butter. Media declared war on Nixon to deepen the Vietnam crisis. This media imperialism in Watergate was closely followed by Congress, and but for the congressional Inquisition so ruthlessly rolling forward, the media onslaught in Watergate would have remained a non-starter. In another system of government, criticism of government during war, and evidently obstructing the war-effort and the war machine is clearly the offence of treason. But in an open democracy like the United States, there exists no offence called treason at present. In the anticlimax of the many wars in the Far East, this criticism hampering the war effort was euologised as the highest form of democratic patriotism, and this kind of patriotism has become the creed of the coward and defeatist. Has the media any special right, other than what has been constitutionally conferred on the ordinary citizen? No. Whether he is journalist or investigative journalist, there is no special constitutional entitlement for him to defame the reputation of another man, but see how things are going on in the United States. All that the journalist and TV man commit is scandal, which is the offence of defamation, exposing themselves to criminal prosecution and claims on civil damages. But court proceedings is another ordeal for the aggrieved plaintiff, whose biography and reputation will be more deeply scandalized, invaded and pulverised by the defendant in an open court, proceedings. Fearing more baseless and false accusations and defamation in the course of a court trial, the poor plaintiff suffers the columny of the journalist, and the electronic media, and again suffers in silence. So, it is only rarely one goes to court to repair his reputation. These are the many questions on the issue of fundamental rights, Bill of Rights, civil rights and privacy laws coming to the rescue of the victim. But the media man, well informed on the techniques and tactics of procedural law, takes on the poor plaintiff who is incapable or facing the barrage of imaginary scandal-bombs, likely to be hurled at him in the open court. Therefore, the victim makes a quick retreat leaving the media-man rule supreme once again. For the American president or British prime minister or any other prime minister in a democracy, it would be strategic disaster to go for a court case to clean up his reputation. If he is assured of success ultimately, the tension, loss of sleep, uncertainty, the coming of new vengeful defaming charges on untrue facts, impressing the credulous and the inimical, then deliberately he has to avoid an open court brawl with his detractors, merely for personal and privacy reasons. This retreat by the victim of defamation, gives a free hand to the media-assailant to come with more powerful attacks. Democracy is yet to devise a defence to defeat this journalistic juggernaut called scandals. Political scandals, in spite of grave opposition by leaders and public, remain irresponsible as well as irrepressible, because the power of defamation is built on deep-rooted malice. Against all existing law, the law of scandals is overgrowing into the new weapon styled "supra-constitutional".

3
Limited Wars Leading To Disasters

America had to face many military failures in the past, and most of these came out of political irresolution and congressional jealousy of the presidency. Separation of powers has been devised to prevent the sabotage of democracy by the powerful executive, as well as by armed forces. In a country like the United States, where the civil authority has been well entrenched, the principle of separation has worked well in peace times. But in national emergencies and crises, this separation-doctrine has worked to bring to the country surrender, humilitation and defeat. Here I will add that this undercutting has been done by the legislature and sometimes by the judiciary too to assert its power on the executive. Again, we shall admit certain basic facts. What is the state machine made of? It is really made of the executive. Only to aid the executive there must be laws and there must be laws only to maintain rule of law. What is the original premise on which the law is made? Law is in support of the policy of the executive. Suppose the executive wants to make primary education free; there must be a law for it as such law alone can make the right a legal one, which can be claimed by all citizens alike. In a parliamentary democracy, the prime minister or the cabinet has no difficulty to legislate any new law in support of its policy, because the prime minister is the leader of the house and his whip runs on all the party members. But in a presidential system the executive getting all his laws passed by the legislature is very rare and this (Congress in USA) legislative opposition is a constant threat on executive power. Even if the President's party controls the American Congress, he is not assured of congressional support, because the party fails to discipline them. In fact the American President has no whip against Congress members. So what emerges at last is a compromise or compromises which defeats the full executive power-play, which is essential for political power.

Undeniable that American leadership of the world is exercised only through the President. But Congress alone has the power to ratify treaties. The failure of the American Congress to ratify the Versailles Treaty led to the exclusion of American power in the League of Nations, and this absence of the most powerful economic and military power led to the collapse of the League, leading to the Second World War. It is sometimes argued that even America becoming a member of the League would not have prevented the catastrophe. This is one argument. However, if America was a member of the League, and she was party to a League resolution against wars, things would have been different. Historians contend that if France had made a firm stand against Hitler in 1936 against the occupation of Sear land the latter would not have occupied it. Then France was having a defeatist military chief called Gamelin, who in spite of possessing the best military machine in Europe, including the best air force, failed to stop Hitler out of irresolution. Also if Britain had made an emphatic declaration that any expansion of German power in Europe including Polish territory will be a cause for war, Hitler would have hesitated. The English warning came, but very late. But once the war machine starts rolling forward, these questions are answered not by leaders, but by the battle field. If France and England had more courageous leaders like Churchill or De Gaulle in 1936, they could have stopped the Hitlerite armageddon in the start itself. Then, the role of America as member of the League would have been more relevant and decisive. But the decisive voice will come only from the mouth of the President and from none else. The Congress could not speak on behalf of America, but it could muffle the voice of the President and so America was pulled out of the mainstream of world affairs in 1921, only due to legislative usurpation of executive power. The legislature is there to harness and discipline the executive, and not to stop it. It is explained that Woodrove Wilson did no home-work in Capitol Hill before starting for Versailles in 1919, and the congressional caucus felt neglected by the reigning president, and the greatest peace treaty in history lay there in shambles. Wilson could assemble the Worlds 'largest gathering of kings', presidents, prime ministers, princes and princesses, counts and dukes and religious chiefs, tribal captains and military marshalls at Versailles and could divide and dismantle three biggest empires, but he fell at the hands of his own Congress. Do the Versailles Treaty and its nonratification by the US Congress and the ensuing diplomatic isolation of the biggest power on earth speak highly of American separation of powers? Congress was more concerned of preserving the prestige of its members rather than the prestige of the nation. The august body was suspicious of the power of its chief executive, and wanted to defeat his policies, and they do not care if American honour is shattered and condemned in the game. On the other hand, if Wilson had been the Prime Minister of America and Congress his parliament with his majority, what would have been the fate of Versailles Treaty? America would have been actively contending with Hitler on his conquest designs, and Hitler would never have jumped upon Poland ignoring the American reaction. We are here looking at the American isolation caused by her separation of powers. America or any other country can exercise her international power-play only through her executive, and when that executive is weakened, it weakens the nation. Had America a parliamentary democracy with a two party system, her leadership of the world would have been more spectacular, decisive and interventionist. But having adopted the law of separation, each branch tries to establish its own primacy, and in the competition, governance suffers. Very often one branch is maintaining a definitive jealousy towards the executive branch and the court system (judiciary) is no exception.

The executive is the real ruler. But the other two branches eye for a share of executive power. An activist court, and what does it do? It wants a share in the policy-making power and this is naked executive power. The court does not stop there. It wants to legislate through judicial decisions, and this encroaches both on the executive and the legislature, and of late the Congress is very much enamoured of having a larger share in the executive power. Congress passed the War Powers Act, and this robs the President of freedom of action in the battle-field. Can the Congress tell the President when to begin firing guns, when to shoot howitzers, when to lob a grenade and when a soldier will fire a missile against the enemy? Can they say when to advance and when to retreat? But through the War Powers Act, the Congress started the ludicrous game of issuing battle-field orders. The congressional quest was once for presidensing, and now it is especially for generalling in the battle field.

Congress does not care if wars possible to be won are abjectly lost. Congress does not care if limited wars lead into unlimited defeats. Congress does not care if a million Vietnam refugees are butchered by communists, these refugees being caught in the cross-fire between Congress and the President. But they are determined to invent petty charges like obstruction of justice and perjury–the offences created and reconstructed in the court-hall only due to the forensic inventiveness of the justice system. What is that the Congress thinks about the leadership of the President and his right to rule? This Power struggle is a permanent nuisance in the American system which can never be got rid of.

It is true that President Bush came to power through an electoral accident and no use in saying that great rulers often come by accident. A careful pre-study of presidential-timber by the public usually fails to make a true career-assessment. Great rulers are born and not made, and they make themselves felt when they reach power. If they fail to get power, the world loses their service, and history provides no credible mechanism by which great rulers are located. Bush came to office in the puzzle of a ballotting accident, which stands as clear discredit to his electoral win. But that is no disqualification for a ruler when he is designated to rule. Great rulers rarely come through popular vote. Alexander The Great came to the throne in a palace revolution (palace conspiracy) in which he joined hands with some of his father's generals and revolted against his father-Philip II. Philip was murdered and the top generals supported Alexander to ascend the throne. The great Alexander coming to power was through patricide, but history records him as one of the greatest of conquerors. We have to take the more recent case of Vietnam. When the historian writes about Vietnam, he will never care to say that it was because of congressional opposition and media indictment of Nixon in Watergate that America failed in Vietnam. On the other hand he will record that America failed because of weak statesmanship, isolationism and battle fear. When America was trounced in Vietnam, its military machine was at its peak, but of what use? Her armed forces remained many times stronger than the enemy, and if so why they surrendered? They surrendered because the American Congress and the media were more inclined to represent the fearfuls and cowards, and they are afraid of war and death, and they terrorised the people by preaching the dangers of war. The great wars ignore journalists. Is there any instance of the media, especially the journalist supporting a courageous political adventurist? It never had been. Wars are won only by the courageous, the brave, and the resolute and not by critics. History records that many wars of democracy are lost because of its argumentative defeatism. If one U.S. soldier dies in Iraq, the American media wails aloud as if no American soldier shall die in any war. But they agree that Americans are not immortal. It is reported that more than ten thousand Iraqis died in the beginning days of Gulf War II, but only about one hundred, and fifty Coalition soldiers died. The proportion is one to one hundred and the most favourable ratio in the history of wars. But the American media wail over the one hundred and fifty dead and they wail perhaps that so few Americans alone died. What is this logic? When we call Alexander the Great the greatest conqueror in history, we never count his dead soldiers in the battlefield. When one Buddhist monk, so crazy about his-martyrdom, self-immolated in Saigon (Now Ho-Chi-Minh city) the world media celebrated it with a sea of tears, as if it a horrendous American offence on humanity. About 55,000

American soldiers died in the Vietnam War, but the fact that the loss on the Vietcong side was many times more, is uncared for and unreported. When democracies are fighting wars for the defence of human freedom, it is pictured and condemned as imperialistic and murderous. If five American soldiers die in Iraq, the media in the free world calls it wasteful martyrdom, and so condemns it. Has the American media ever condemned the mass-killings of innocents by Saddam? Saddam killed his entire political establishment in a single act of slaughter, and he came out supreme. He killed 5000 Kurds by poison gas and all died in minutes. Was there any call by the media that this atrocity should be punished? Even on Idi Amin–the cruellest despot with wild ferocity, the media had no complaint. If the Ugandan media were afraid of his reprisals, then why the outside media men fear him? Media men never proclaim themselves as pro-dictator or pro-totalitarian or antidemocratic but their conduct helps only those people. Democracy gets strong rulers like Bush only rarely, but the media men and the investigative journalists are determined to demolish and destroy the regime of strong democratic rulers. Now it is the vested right of the media to promote only incapable and weak rulers in democracies. When they want to destroy the strong, their weapon is scandal. Scandals are the job of the gossiper, the tale carrier, the court-fool and the broker but it is the media man who does it now to condemn. This is the curse of democracy, but no remedy is found against these media-sinners, self-styling as a media-puritans.

Bush being a strong President the media is bound to dislike him. That dislike is so intense that a media-war is declared against the President, the moment it is found that he is not compliant. Media wants to establish that if a President wants to rule, he must submit to the regimen issued by the media mughals and journalists. And their new weapon is the most immorally developed one-investigative journalism and its effluence–the-scandal. President Bush, while in office, is not a Clinton like women chaser, and first of all he wanted to break new ground by inventing a sex-free Presidency even if running the risk of becoming a mesogynist. Against this precaution, the investigative journalist including Wood Ward and Bernstein will be greatly angry and now they have to invent new causes, and they go to the moral fall of defending Saddam Hussein, the murderer of hundreds of thousands, perhaps just below Stalin, Hitler and Mao Zedong. They say that there is no judicial evidence like proof on the existence of weapons of mass destruction (WMD) in Iraq, and Bush lied to the nation. FDR won the Second World War. Will any one be silly enough to say that FDR lied to the people and misled the Allies by mispronouncing the name of a soldier and later forgetting the name it self? What meaningless, careless, purposeless exercise is the media and the Congress engaged in? The purpose of going to war is victory in the battlefield. America and Bush won the Iraq war, and Saddam has been overthrown, captured, and custodied. He is readied for trial under a special tribunal. The surrender committed in 1990 by Sr. Bush under his general Collin Powell is not repeated now. But the media, as the errand boy of a rebellious Congress (I say American Congress is a perpetual rebellion against the President) is running about in search of new causes. The media and the Congress fail deliberately to endorse the reality of an American military victory, and again fail to recognise that the most virulent and genocidal dictator has been overthrown, and ground made ready for founding a democratic government in Iraq. The revolting media is trying to invent cases and causes only to lay siege on the presidency, and the new reasons are failure to discover WMD and the failure to prevent the 11/9 disaster. True, Al Qaeda made numerous threats, and many threats shall be red-herrings to mislead. Plane hijackings, car bombings, suicide bombings, mass killing of innocents in crowded places, and a hundred dubious acts are done by the terrorist to surprise and mislead the preventive steps. The Congress started an enquiry, and a commission has been appointed to investigate whether September/11 could have been prevented. Of all the words of tongue and pen, the most pitiable is that it might have been, but the foolish hunt on the prevention steps continues in the most celebrated way. Credibility of American democracy, in its colonial enterprises, has been very high as a liberator. American democracy was expanding in the 19th century and she captured Philippines and Mexico. Louisiana was purchased on payment of money to the cash-starved Napoleon Bonaparte. Alaska was purchased, again on payment of cash to the Russian Czar who believed that it is a land inaccessible and in-hospitable to the Russian population, who are very thinly distributed in the vast homeland. Then came, the turn of the Spanish-American War 1898 which gave U.S. possession of New Mexico and Texas. The lands, which are adjoining or integral are incorporated to the union and these are Texas, Alaska, Louisiana, New Mexico etc. The original states of 13 have grown into 50, and US was getting into continental shape. Philippines was granted independence and she is an American ally though not a steadfast one. In Central America, countries like Cuba, Panama, Guatemala, Nicaragua etc. were, under virtual American domination for long periods. The Panama Canal was built by US under the resolute leadership of Theodore Roosevelt, and after running it for nearly a century it was handed over to Panamanians. But America could have easily incorporated these states into the Union if she wanted them, and her military supremacy for more than a century warrants this possibility. If Hawaii, lying deep into the Pacific Ocean, can be the 49th state of the Union and Alaska the remote snowy wilderness the 50th , then why not Panama, Cuba and Nicaragua? May be America never wanted to colonise or annex these territories.

At present the political debate of the world centres on American bad conduct in the World, ignoring her good conduct. After its conquest in the 19th century, Philippines was granted freedom in 1946. But the spectacular American concession to world nationalism came after the Second World War. At the conclusion of the war, the whole of Western Europe, Italy, Greece etc. were under American domination and Allied occupation. Roosevelt failed grievously at Yalta to understand the Stalinist designs on Europe and so because of FDR's neglect Eastern Europe went to Russian occupation and regimentation. This Russian annexation made through betrayal and lies was overthrown only in the mass uprisings of 1989. The Russian terror in Eastern Europe was the result of the careless handling of the negotiation at Yalta and FDR was blamed that his delegation to Yalta included many Russian spies who manipulated the negotiations and its terms. But Eastern Europe would have been saved of the terror and tragedy if FDR did not hand over Eastern Europe to Stalin on a platter. It is a sad, tragic story to be retold, but it is a story to re-educate the nationalists of Europe too. Then what did America do with territories occupied by Allied forces? It was, Germany who started the war in full collaboration with Russia. Germany failed but Russia succeeded because Russia switched sides midway because of the murderous designs of Adolf Hitler on Russia and Bolshevism. Hitler, who started World War II in 1939 with the attack on Poland, suddenly turned against Russia in 1941, and invaded his comrade in arms. Stalin was warned by many about Hitler's plans but he did not believe, those gossips and so he was surprised of Barbarossa (The German attack of Russia so code named). When it came on him, Stalin was thrown into the Allied camp abruptly and this was great relief to Winston Churchill. Allies came to Russia's rescue and that alliance did not break-up midway and continued till the conclusion of war. After the war and triumph when the spoils were divided, Eastern Europe went to Russian occupation and western Europe including in the Norwegian peninsula came under Allied control.

Once the war concluded and the Allies emerged victorious, the first American concern was the immediate liberation and return of territory to its people and not perpetuation of occupation. However, Europe lay in shambles and so the immediate task of America was to send a huge relief package to alleviate the war-time sufferings of the people and restore the population into a society of law and order. That they did it immediately and won the confidence of the occupied people. The free world was lucky that in spite of the whopping and crushing war expenses, the American economy remained dynamic and resourceful to finance the reconstruction of the whole of Europe unoccupied by Russia, and very soon these countries–Italy, Germany, France, Belgium, etc.—were reorganised to grow into self-sufficiency and self-reliance. It was the legendary Marshall Plan of President Truman that prevented Europe from economic collapse and communist take over. In 1948, countries like Greece and Italy were in political turmoil, but with effective American intervention, and to some extent because of peoples' discipline, prevented these two crucial Mediterranean states from falling to communism. The former mayor of Bonn-Konrad Adeneur was picked up to represent the Germans, and a German democracy was organised and in 1949 sovereign status was granted to West Germany. West Germany under Adeaneur soared to new economic heights and now the unified Germany is the most powerful economy in Europe. She can be today the most powerful military power of Europe also who, like Japan is also under ban from rearming, but her defence forces and the German contingent in NATO are very powerful units. What was then in 1945 preventing America from converting Germany, France, Greece, Italy etc. into American colonies? Certainly continued occupation will bring resistance from nationalists and a civil war for liberation will be the result. Then for an imperial coloniser, is the prospect of a possible civil war a deterrent? Russia occupied the huge territory of eastern Europe which comprised East Germany, Austria, Czechoslovakia, Poland, Latvia, Estonia, Lithuania, Hungary, Rumania and Bulgaria and clung on to these territories until 1989, when the Soviet empire itself broke up. There were massive uprisings and bloody resistances in these lands, but every revolt was quelled by Soviet armour. The 1954 uprising in East Germany hoped for an American rescue operation, but that rescue team never came, and like the Polish Ghetto uprising it was bloodily suppressed by Soviet tanks. The Hungarian uprising of 1956 is the continuing testimony to the murderous ways of Russian suppression, when more than 20,000 unarmed Hungarian revolters were shot dead in the streets of Budapest alone. This invited worldwide protests and condemnation, but the bloody end of the revolt sent the message to future revolters and liberators that against the armed might of the modern state, there is no possible remedy. Then came the Czech Spring of 1968, which again was repeating the bloody end for revolters. Therefore, with effective and merciless use of army, nowadays the chance for success of such revolts is very rare. Arms can be countered by arms that are more dangerous, but the experience of Eastern Europe says that it is very difficult to defeat the armed power of a totalitarian state. The main reason is that the totalitarian system is in human and remorseless. The means of production are wholly under state control and therefore the revolters have no independent means to buy arms or finance civil wars. On the other hand, in a free society, anyone has his own independent means, and therefore the opportunities for converting these means and resources into war expenses or war equipment are full. When the Soviet-juggernaut could quell the massive uprisings in East Germany, and Czechoslovakia and the thousands of undeclared revolts in other parts of Eastern Europe, and maintain and perpetuate anti-people rulers of massive corruption and accumulated personal wealth , what was not the opportunity for America to convert Western Europe, Italy, Greece etc, into American colonies and hold on to it? It is true that under the stress and strain of colonisation, the spectacular economic progress and national consolidation achieved by these countries would have been impossible, but who among the colonial overlords want their subject people to grow prosperous and live prosperous? The colonial master never want the subject to became rich and strong, but America helped its occupied subjects to grow into rich democracies, at the highest speed possible. This is the story of post war non communist Europe.

Now Germany and France have grown so powerful that they never more are the yes-men of America. A Europe, which is free and prosperous, cannot be expected to be a compliant American ally, as compliance and endorsement comes out of necessities and never out of morals. Before 1989, Europe was under the shadow of a Soviet nuclear strike, and the French and British strike forces were not a match for the Russian spearhead. So Germany, France and the free Europe wanted to live under American nuclear umbrella. If a nuclear war is not preferred by Russia, then there remained the massive threat of the armour of the Warsaw Pact powers, a euphemism for Soviet imperial forces. For any nation, survival is her first need and to succeed to survive they had to toe the American line. But then comes the sudden collapse of Soviet Union and the grand-demolitionist had been Michael Gorbachev. Gorbachev pulled down the Iron Curtain and called the world to come and see Russia's deplorable, paralyzed existence, under a retro growth economy. The Russian system could no more carry on like a state. There was an attempted military coup to foil this grand demolition but that failed. Thus the champion of world revolution collapsed, and the Marxian arcadia lay there in debris. The Iron Curtain was pulled down and the misery and want of the people of Russia and Eastern Europe lay there bare for the naked eye to see. Now the only communist country in the world is China. The Cold War ended and Western Europe no more needs the protection of the American nuclear umbrella. France and Germany have come to an un-American judgment on Iraq. They say America going to war in Iraq is wrong. But these countries said in 1991 that Saddam, who unleashed an unprovoked aggression on Kuwait should be severely punished. But now, they speak a different voice and the reasons are more domestic than international. The German Chancellor, Gerhard Schroeder was facing a re-election, which was surely to pack him home unless he is able to perform a political somersault. The German opinion was against going to war in Iraq. He made a sudden about-turn to make a retreat and questioned the political wisdom of going against Saddam, and the moral right of the United States to do it now. If America had asked the moral question, then the Morgentheau Plan would have been accepted by America in 1945 to convert Germany into a pastoral society. The question, which America did not ask to Germany at the end of Second World War, is now coldly and thanklessly resurrected by Schroeder simply to win an election. When Charles De Gaulle, came to power again in 1958, he immediately made a revolt in the NATO camp challenging American supremacy and he wanted the American NATO units to vacate French territory. This was a terrible blow to the unity of NATO when Cold War tensions have peaked, and strategists were contending on the consequences of a nuclear armageddon between United States and Soviet Union. De Gaulle immediately started the scheme to join the nuclear club and speedily developed a modest independent nuclear strike force. The U.S. administration was awfully struck by this French volte face, but De Gaulle was determined to furrow an independent French foreign policy-line, which for the first time wanted to make accommodation with Russia. Now, De Gaulle becomes more acceptable to Kremlin. What was the reason for this French volte face in NATO? Some say the French are bitter that America failed to rescue them in Indo-China, and Eisenhower and John Foster Dulles turned a deaf year to their frantic pleas for help. During Indo-China war, it was not De Gaulle who was in office. But the French humiliation especially at Dien Bien Phu was devastating the French morale as a whole. The French wanted to retain Indo-China, but America vetoed the idea. Winston Churchill, the then British Premier, who could never come to terms with a British empire without Indian told bluntly that if the British will not fight to keep India for them, he does not think they will fight to keep Indo-China for the French. But it is more the evidence of a thankless face of De-Gaulle who was obsessed with the glory of France as a great power. But De Gaulle was a realist also and came to the truth of the futility of resisting the Algerian revolt, though more than four million French are settled in that colony. The day of reckoning makes it clear that it was the American free society and her transparency that forced the dissolution of the British, French and Dutch empires. FDR never favoured colonisation by Britain, France and other European countries though he was chiefly responsible for the expansion of Russia into Eastern Europe and the Baltic States. While dismantling the English, French and the Spanish empires, FDR and Truman abetted the sudden rise and expansion of a new empire–the communist empire. Luckily, India was saved from the tentacles of red expansion mainly because of the Himalayan barrier, a strong national movement under Gandhi and due to a well-knit administration system left in tact by the British. But even after the Sovietisation of Eastern Europe, the loss of China to communism was the biggest setback to Asian freedom. Even then if FDR or Truman stood for another term, they would have won hands down. Military failures and diplomatic disasters do not make a dent in the popularity of American Presidents as it does now also. On the moral plane, it is the real triumph of America to have over-thrown Saddam Hussein. In fact, the Iraqi people are liberated and they are now being re-organised to reach the stage of self-determination. But in between, there are dark forces in the Arab world who see liberation and self-rule as un-Islamic, and that is the cause and catalyst for violence. Iraq, among the Arabs, is a civilisation of many millennia, and in that history, democracy has never been a ruler's idea. It is this lack of ideals that prompt them for violence and this violence is generally in the nature of a war to capture power, that is never built on the ideals of democracy. Here craze for personal power is projected under the cloak of religious fundamentalism. It is difficult to explain the motives of the Middle East rulers, but an undeniable motive is the absolute claim for power, one way or other. The Zambian President, sent his army to Uganda to overthrow the murderous regime of the dictator - Idi-Amin and the latter toppled and forced out of the country. Idi Amin was the cruellest dictator then alive in the world–but he was the Ugandan ruler who came to power in a military coup and continued his terror for several years letting loose a bloody reign that kept the nation under his thumb. He shot many thousands of his innocent people and all suspected opponents and the Asian immigrants were forced to leave the country at gun-point under threat of rape, forced labour, etc. India did not intervene to protect the large Indian community there, because it is against international law. However, is there any protection against inhuman terror, genocide, and torture under international law? NATO intervened militarily in Kosovo and Serbia but under what law? America intervened in Kuwait in 1991, and battled the first Gulf War and under what law? Under what law, outsiders intervened in the Spanish Civil War? Russians intervened and crushed the Hungarian revolt of 1956 and under what law? America intervened in Guatemala and Nicaragua but under what law? America entered Panama and constructed the Panama Canal? What was the law and moral that sanctioned the American intervention in Afghanistan that caused the overthrow of Taliban? We can cite from history hundreds of cases of uncalled for military intervention in other states, and all these had been blatant breaches of international law. Interventions are made because it is militarily possible to intervene and the intervener thinks that his self-interest forces him to do so and it is not unduly risky and dangerous. In the case of Iraq, America took a beating in the 1991 war, and the people of the United States felt that their President has made an unnecessary, uncalled for surrender. Therefore, George Bush Jr. wanted to undo that damage and decided on a second conquest of Iraq. The overthrow of Saddam was more easier possible this time, and the emaciated Saddam living underground near Tikrit has been captured. Perhaps his confidants cheated him and that is the way rulers are sold out. Success came too soon for George W. Bush, and his popularity soared to unprecedented heights. Yes, he won the war his father had lost, and America acclaims it. But one year after the war, his popularity ratings are low and what are the reasons damaging his reputation? Because the media says that the American President has lied and misled the nation? A vituperative media is inventing reasons to discredit a victory that America very much desired and wanted.

In 1991, the American people defeated Bush Sr., in re-election because they believed he lost the war. In 2004, the same American people are planning and conspiring to defeat Bush Jr. who won the war and brought glory for American democracy. A sad commentary on modern history that the media man, particularly the journalist , does not like strong rulers. Once losing a war was the reason for unpopularity and defeat, but now winning the war is the reason. Quite surprising to know that democracy has no firm morals to proclaim and rely on. Who can save a democracy who accuses the winner and the loser with equal uneasiness and intolerance! This is the dark side of American democracy that forces many failures on the nation. If the American power, both economic and military, had been deployed with alertness and courage, a lot of miseries of the world and many tragedies of humanity could have been averted. In spite of being the most powerful economic and military force on earth, as master of the huge military industrial complex, she remains a democracy and every four years she elects a person as President, many of whom are incapable. Rarely she gets a Bush Jr. or a Reagan but most are Carters and Fords.

4
American Defeatism Riding On Scandals

American military power is the bulwark of the free world. If the American media and the Congress think, on the basis of her national territories and borders, the free world, stand threatened. America went to war for the sake of human freedom on most occasions. When Roosevelt brought victory for the Allies, it was really a victory guaranteeing the future freedom of man. But that victory was at the cost of hundreds of thousands of American dead and many more wounded. The American media in those days did not complain that American soldiers were dying in the battle fields of the world, and such loss of life had been wastefully inflicted on the nation by a trigger-happy President, and that too for the safety and freedom of others. History gives us enough logic to argue that if America could remain truly neutral in the European war against Hitler, and desisted from assisting the Allies with economic help and lend lease, there would have been no need for her to go to war against the Axis. It is questionable too whether the war against Japan was unavoidable. The American partiality towards China was the Achilles heel in the pre-war Japanese relations with the United States, and the Japanese resented that their drive for more space in Manchuria is viewed as a hostile act by the United States.

The Japanese militarists could have been dissuaded from adventure, if there was American accommodation in Manchuria. Manchuria was not a strategic spot as far as American defence needs in the Far East were concerned. Some still ask whether the Japanese strike on Pearl Harbour in 1941 was not without justification. But like George W Bush, if FDR was really concerned about the lives of American soldiers liable to be lost in a flare up of the conflagration in the Far East, and the American people eager to accuse him of war-mongering, leading to his electoral defeat, what would FDR do then? He would suddenly pull back into abject isolation. But the pre-World War II America was not a home of defeatists. If for aiding the European war effort and for responding to the strike at Pearl Harbour, FDR was faced with the prospect of a clear defeat at the next poll (World War II lasted 6 years and FDR was elected four times) would he be going for war at all? Never, because loss of office means loss of power and slipping into oblivion, while the war, which he started, will be going on at somebody else's command. If war and victory meant certain defeat at the polls, the American President would have remained a spectacular observer of the European tragedy, insensitive to the fate of humanity and human rights. And what would be the result?- America capitulates and the free world endangered.

To remain a superpower for long will be extremely boring for America because suddenly she is faced with a world that offers no challenges. Now the people of America are brainstormed by the super-state's media, advocating anti-state policies and isolationism. They accuse the President that Americans are dying in Iraq- but only in small members. Iraq is under occupation by Anglo-American forces and the transfer of power is subject to the occupier's supervision. The Iraqis are slowly turning into guerrilla fighters, in spite of all promises for early pull out and exit of foreign troops. But terrorists are jubilant when they get maximum publicity in the electronic media. When five American soldiers die in Iraq, at least ten times more Iraqis also die. But the media asks why American soldiers also die in a shooting war. Shooting is to kill and this is applicable to Americans also. The present argument of the United States media is that America can go to war but they must wage it without American casualties, and what a fantastic plea? The Congress too joins issue. That America has to wage her wars without casualities is like Portia asking Shylock to take a pound of flash from the body without shedding a drop of blood. In the 20th and 21st centuries, all important American wars are likely to be for the defense of others. Take World War I-it was for the defence of Europe and not for the defence of America; Second World War for the defence of the free world. The war in Korea was to stop the conquest of South Korea by communist China and North Korea. The war in Vietnam was for preventing the conquest of South Vietnam by the North; the massive airlift of life support articles during the Berlin Blockade was to prevent the fall of West Berlin to Russia. Then comes the guerrilla War in Afghanistan which ultimately ended in the withdrawal of Russia from that country. The historic occasion comes when Saddam Hussein invaded Kuwait in 1989. Then within no time one of the formidable Coalition forces was organised involving Europe, North America, Australia, Japan and NATO. But that ended in American magnanimity and George W.H Bush surrendered before Saddam Hussein. Come September/11, 2001, the whole political scene in the west, undergoes a revolution and America vows on revenge on this terrible slaughter of innocents. This revenge is called the Second Gulf War. The first target was Afghanistan-where the fundamentalist Taliban was harbouring all terrorists, rampaging world wide. Reputed that the King of Al Qaeda-Osama Bin Laden is hiding in the white mountains of Afghanistan. The Taliban could be driven from the countryside, but part of the country is still under their control. It is the Afghan people who now govern (non-govern) the country under the care of American supporting forces and immediate elections are planned. The great question that now haunts President Bush, in his electoral campaign, is the war in Iraq. When a country goes to war, the concern of the patriot is whether the war is won or lost. Once you win the war, the ruler who led the battle is coming back as a national hero. But in the political misinformation campaign in the United States the hero is called the villain. What a distortion of facts, history and national honour? The United States media does not like an American victory anywhere in the world, because the media does not like America succeed. The media wants to mount the victory band-wagon, but war provide no opportunity for them for front-line duties. History has the story of thousands of wars, and triumphs, celebrated as national, honours. But the media and the Congress, in order to belittle and tarnish the image of the President, are running about to find excuses for robbing the President of his achievements. One such charge is that the President, went to war without sufficient justification as Saddam Hussein has turned into an honourable man having no WMD in hands. With no WMD in hands, he shall be a political gentleman, when Bush Jr. invaded his beloved country. When Saddam is venerated around the world for his Arabian heroics, waging a war against him is like waging a war against angel. True American Congress is hunting the President and the President in on the run, especially when he is facing re-election as the most controversial person on earth. The moral ground for the war non-existent, the victory shall be immoral and so the media contends. There was no such unpatriotic media in Europe or America during and after the Second World War. Otherwise, these sin-chasers would have grilled FDR and Truman that the moral ground for a just war did not exist and therefore the territories taken from Hitler are to be returned to his descendants. What demeaning logic the media is digging up to supply the president hunters in the Congress! Wars are started because the attacker believes that he will win, and all other reasons and conditions are subordinated to this hope for victory. Conquerors give different reasons for each attack. Again take the example of Hitler. He gave one reason against Czechoslovakia and Austria and, then against Poland, Belgium, Norway, France and again against Bulgaria, Rumania and Hungary different treasons, and finally against Russia another reason, and it goes on like that. Can any one in the world give any importance to these statements? No, only futile to search for the moral justifications of wars already fought and won or fought and lost. Is there a more deplorable, and wasteful enquiry than looking into the causes that led to a war? People go to war because war is in the great tradition, said J.B Priestley, and that logic applies irresistibly in the case of all wars, whether it is the wars of Alexander, Napoleon, Hitler or George W. Bush. In the Iraq war the end frelly justifies the means.

The journalist's prejudices compel him not to concede that it is the President or the Prime Minister who led the nation to war and victory. On the other hand the newsman starts his diabolic hunt when the war is lost. When there is defeat, there will be cry for the blood of the ruler who went to war and even if a dictator, a defeat often brings him down from power. But in that respect also Saddam is an exception, having no political second line of succession left alive. America had to make a second attempt for his overthrow. Saddam rule was despotic, and he is a mass killer. He started an unprovoked war on Iran and caused the death of a million people and untold sufferings for his own people as well as to the enemy. He was the messiah of death and destruction. He murdered Kurds in thousands as they challenged his authority. He imagined himself into a Second Alexander the Great and was blind enough to believe that even great powers were weaker than he. Killing was his favourite past time, and he enjoyed it. What did he do for Iraq, for the Arab world , for Islamic fundamentalism and for the people at large? To all he supplied agony, cruelty, misery and want. The large battery of his supporters who laboured day and night to install him in power were wholly shot in a night operation whose cruelty, fraud, misrepresentation and ruthlessness could not be matched even by Stalin. Stalin at least gave a show trial for his party-men who were suspected as working against him. Stalin's was also a process extending to many years, and called the Great Purge. But Saddam committed the mass purge immediately on seizing power. When all his supporters were killed, his Baath party power pyramid had no base and apex. Enjoying unrestrained, arbitrary power, he had fantastic visions of conquest, annexation and empire building and went on unleashing terror on all and everywhere. But he lost the Iran War, and to compensate the loss and humiliation, he pounced upon the rich but defenceless brother country called Kuwait. Kuwait is a wealthy country with a lots of petro-dollars in her coffers, but maintaining no defence forces, with a very strange self confidence. Kuwait had neglected the fact that without armed strength at its command she cannot defend her territory. But she is pro-western and could bank on western help, but how can she be sure that in the actual hour of danger, American forces will come to her rescue? And even if America comes, what is the guarantee that western forces and especially the defeatists in the American Congress will not force her into an unseemly, unacceptable compromise? So Kuwait has to create a credible defence force. If she does not have the necessary population strength to recruit locally, she can recruit an army from another Arab country; and if an Arab army is suspect she can recruit an army from any Asian or African country and these recruits, being emigres and replaceable, will pose no threat for the rulers. But though the development of a police force has somewhat progressed, Kuwait is yet to formulate a programme for self defence forces. She has enough money to build a defence force, and then why she refuses to build one of her own? With enough means at hand, it is unwise for her to live a defenceless life. The rulers of Kuwait must look to the example of Singapore–a country of only 200 square miles having a defence force of its own. It is not always safe to depend on others for national security. When the American President is a fickle soul like Ford or Carter, what would have been Kuwait's fate?

The tragedies that the world had to face because of the isolationism and the congress-president feud have been innumerable. A President went to war in Iraq, and he came back with victory. Now the next question is whether to colonise Iraq or handover power to Iraqis. Bush has only one plan and that is to hand over, and never to colonise. Anglo-American powers handed over power to Iraq on 27th June 2004, and declared that America has no intention to colonise Iraq, much less exploit the limitless oil resources of that country to

America's advantage. An Interim Governing Council comprising Iraqis alone has been set up. The American' s are there to oversee the transition to full democracy. But democracy is still not an attractive term in the Arab World who honour only Kings, dictators and terrorists. They heed to the call of fundamentalists, and neglect the code of democracy, and that is the basic problem with the Iraqis also. Once America declared her intention to hand over power to Iraqis, and promised free and fair elections in the very near future, when law and order is fully restored, what is the logic of the Iraqi violence, which the world media want to celebrate as liberation war? If they want freedom at the earliest, then self-rule is very near, but self-rule cannot be anarchy. Though dictators alone ruled Iraq after the British had left, there was no anarchy and collapse of the security apparatus till the war. But tomorrow if the Coalition Forces leave Iraq all on a sudden, what will be the condition of the country? There will immediately be fighting, erupting, and leading the country into a civil war between Shias, Sunnies and Kurds etc. Kurds will revolt for their own separate homeland also. Should America quit Iraq without making alternative arrangements for stability and order?

One of the reasons for the success of Indian democracy is the way the British handed over power to an established, well-organised government. It must go to the credit of Indian leaders also for their agreement with the British and doing nothing that would disturb an orderly transfer of power. It was a transfer which must be a model to the world when India had to suddenly face partition of the country into two, and the massive killing's and blood-shed that followed. In fact the Interim Government of 1946 was a government on probation that readied Indian leaders to wrestle with the power of the state. There was complete agreement between the British government and Indian leaders and every issue was negotiated and settled and when the British left, India was under the control of the new leadership. The bureaucracy, the military and the government machinery were smoothly absorbed into the free state. But if the leaders had risen rebellious, and challenged the British at the fag end of their rule, civil war would have been the result. When America is willing to hand over power to Iraqis, what prevents the latter from accepting that handover in an orderly way? When the time-frame for full-hand-over is negotiable, why do the media in the free world (media is free only in the free world) celebrate the violence? The aim of the rebellious Iraqis is something else. The media want to prove that all American efforts to make a free Iraq have failed, and they don't want a peaceful Iraq on the road to progress. Is this their service to Iraqi people? Have not the journalists developed a vested interest in preventing an orderly transfer of power in Iraq? They never admit that they want Iraq to be ruled by a syndicate of terrorists. But what they actually want is disorder and they spread the story that the Anglo-American forces have miserably failed in Iraq. General Giap–the grand-old-man of the Vietminh triumph at Dien Bieu Bhu, comes to warn America that Iraq can be their Second Vietnam and so move cautiously. All these celebrities want to predict the past that American schemes are fundamentally flawed and it fails anywhere in the globe. Is this plea for the good of Iraq and her people? The world media is committed to see America vanquished everywhere, and in this respect the American media also is no exception. The power of the press, the TV and the radio are the power of their monopoly on information-transmission, and not the power of its truth. It has become the political fashion for American media to attack the power of America and the free-world and they don't care if thereby they destroy the power of human rights itself.

The argument against America is that she violated international law by invading Afghanistan and Iraq. No doubt, international law stands violated. When China attacked Tibet and Korea, was not international law violated? When Russia attacked Hungary in 1956, and Czechoslovakia in 1968, was not international law violated? When North Vietnam attacked South Vietnam, was not international law violated? The two Vietnams–North and South were created at the end of protracted negotiations at Geneva, in 1954, and these countries are the product of an international agreement, which both the communist world and the free world jointly approved. But before the inks are dry, the North sent its guerrillas to the South to terrify and terrorise the people there, who were enjoying a great amount of freedom in property and right of expression. This guerrilla war was the result of blatant aggression by North Vietnam, but the world media called it liberation war, and surprisingly that appellation stuck. Against this attempted military takeover of the South by the North, America stepped in and gradually increased her military role into high and mighty. When the North unleashed a wholesale war, America entered the fray with larger forces, but never attempted to gain decisive edge and superiority over the enemy forces by a thorough strategy. The terror tactics of killing, torturing and dismembering the innocent population to frighten them away from the government were practised first by the North Vietnamese against the South, and the population in the South lived frightened. These terror tactics gave the message to the population that if they spoke for the quitting of American forces from Vietnam, they will be taken care of by the self-styled liberators–the Vietcong. People in villages had been coerced into submission before the Vietcong and these people loudly pleaded for the withdrawal of American forces. The people of Vietnams were threatened to believe that for all their misery and sorrow the Americans were responsible. True, like the loss of China, the American people were not ready to fight a winning war and the reasons for this disastrous retreat can be traced to the defeatism and surrender-mania of the American Congress. For the fault of not fighting a full war, America will have to fight many more wars in future.

5
Domestic Revolt Against Wars, Enemy-Sponsored

Congress wants to have a share in the power of the executive and now jealously wants it, but that being not allowed under the Constitution, the petty congressional sovereigns go for statute making, to transfer parts of executive power from the White House to Capitol Hill. If Congressmen annex part of the executive power, they have no execution machinery to use it, and thus the newly pocketed executed power will make their pockets heavier than they. Congress does not know how to play with this power, and therefore this unnatural surgical severance of power from the presidency turns into an act of vengeance against the power of the executive. Right from the days of the republic, the coordination functions between the three departments–the judiciary, the executive and the legislature, has never been clearly defined, and rather impossible to define also, as done in parliamentary governments. Because of separation of powers, every independent branch wants to claim a share in the powers of the other two branches and the separate branches are perpetually at war on the question of overlapping powers. Sometimes these wars are fiercer than foreign wars with enemies, and the American political muscle gets tired in this wasteful game of jealousy wars. This is the reason America could not control the destiny of the world, which she is physically and politically capable of doing.

If the American presidential decisions had been as absolute and final and as that of prime ministers, there would have been no Second World War. The reader may be astonished at this startling contention, but the logic is simple. If America could win World War I and World War II, with much less labour and design, she could have prevented these catastrophes by engaging in preventive force deployments and active diplomacy. Especially during the Second World War an American policy statement that any attempt by Adolf Hitler to invade any other part of Europe will meet with immediate military intervention by America. But as a thirsty onlooker enjoying a bloody duel, America was looking on, and she decides to intervene only after the European blood was almost shed on battle fields, and the human toll reaching many millions. The President is the ruler to order a military intervention, but it is the Congress who holds the money for feeding and equipping the armed forces. FDR from the start of the war, was inclined to go to the aid of Allies who did not jump into the cauldron to conquer. These programmes were for self-defence or for the defence of the defenceless. If FDR was the prime minister of America supported by a parliamentary majority, he could have threatened Hitler with an ultimatum and Hitler could have been stopped. All the Hitlerite hopes were built on the question of American neutrality, and he believed that the Second World War is essentially a European War, in which America need not be concerned. It is contended that France had a parliamentary government then, but those short-term prime ministers were only apologetic to the German superiority, and this cowardice and indecisiveness only emboldened Hitler's adventures. Some Paris newspapers sang flatteries to the Nazi dictator but only on receiving huge bribes, but still a determined French prime minister could have stopped Hitler. The French were all demoralised by their military chief–Gamelin who was traitorously defeatist and pleaded out all prime ministers from the military option. These are the–ifs of the history of prime ministers involved in the Second World War, but there are other baffling questions also. FDR, as president was determined to help the Allies, but he had to cultivate and reconstruct public opinion for an American intervention. The President had to attempt several conciliation moves with Congress, but in spite of these efforts, without the Pearl Harbour strike by Japan, it was improbable that America would have fully entered the war on the side of Allies. American administration always works under severe constraints imposed by Congress, and in many foreign wars the President will not go for intervention, if Congress is unlikely to support him. But the sad situation is that the Congress, due to inter-department jealousy will not concede anything that will enhance the standing of the President, and more so if he belongs to the opposite party of the congressional majority. What an unfortunate situation for a ruler to face! Congress will not hesitate to venture into a conspiracy with the media, especially with the investigative journalist, and prepare a scheme to sabotage presidential programmes. This is the biggest problem a president of the United States is now facing. If George W. Bush is held very high by the world as liberator, the Congress and the media attempt to disclaim and devalue those achievements. Can America overcome this congressional prejudice? But if George W. Bush is the prime minister, he need not even consult the parliamentary party before going to war, as and the parliamentary majority, simply follows him. Now the terrorism war is raging in Iraq, and in war Americans are bound to stand behind the president for victory. Though the liberator of Iraq can be mis-called 'conqueror', the attempt of the American media is to cause one more American defeat and humiliation in the midst of victory, and they lean towards the terrorists. An American humiliation not only in Iraq, but in every battle-field including Korea and Vietnam had unfortunately been the pleasure of American media, and Bush complains that the media does not want an American victory in Iraq. In another country including a parliamentary democracy, any attempt to sabotage a national victory will be considered treason, which again is an offence against the state. The prime minister has much less difficulty than the president in giving tough treatment to treasonable acts. But the American president cannot do it because many treason-like proposals and propositions come from the legislative branch itself, called Congress. When America goes to war all kinds of criticism against the errors, mistakes, horrors and law violations committed by soldiers in the battle field originate either from the Congress or from the media, and under congressional umbrella, the opponents of the president take up the issue to lash out against war efforts. The Congress media combine does not care a damn whether America is losing the war, due to this criticism.

The rights of any citizen and any class of citizens is the same under law, giving equal protection. How the media man can a claim that he is certified to have a special right which the ordinary man does not have? When an ordinary man criticises war and incite opinion against it, it is an unpatriotic act, and when it damages the war effort, it is an offence against the state. But the America Congress criticises American wars abroad without exception, and this criticism is not an in-house criticism as it happens in a parliament debate. Even members of the ruling party may criticize the war, war-policies and war strategy, but once the government is on war, the opposition as well as the members of the ruling party have to support the government policy, whether they like it or not. A conscientious objector of wars in a country is good politics, but bad law when the war is in progress. But what do American Congress do? They openly oppose the President's commands in a war; they openly challenge presidential orders and prepare measures to defeat the war's progress. Congress denies arms to the war-front by denying funds; Congress orders the reduction of forces which may lead to the failure of America in the battle field ; Congress places hurdles on strategies and tactics in combat operations, which restrains America's battling capacity but enables enemy progress. It is to prevent such sabotages from within, that the offence of treason and sedition have been enacted and maintained in the statute book from time immemorial. But the American Congress not only criticises the 'presidents' policies, but they indirectly aid the enemy by open criticism and enjoy an enemy-victory as they enjoyed such victories in Korea and Vietnam. The question is how can America win a war when the national legislature itself is fighting hard to defeat the President who is the prosecutor of all wars? Evidently Congress being the law-maker has no machinery to executive a war. Otherwise, the hundreds of petty sovereigns in the Congress would have no hesitation to legislate transferring the power of war from the hands of the President to the hands of Congress and to re-appoint some one in the House, as the new commander-in-chief. Congress revolting against the presidency is a clear demand for his overthrow. In the United States the constitutional process proceeds in reverse order, but on the mistaken belief that separation of powers condones these wrongs. Separation of powers is good principle but bad administration. When the Congress is fighting a proxy war on behalf of the enemy, why should the journalist lag far behind? Following the Congress way, why not the journalist also attempt to halt his country's war process is a new challenge, misnamed as intellectual challenge, and he becomes the hero in the enemy camp. This political strategy assumes a new name and style, in democracy. During the Nixon Presidency, when the Vietnam War was in progress numerous campus revolts were mounted throughout America and the people behind the revolts had been identified as communists, blacks and the civil liberties activists. Nixon was claiming that these revolts are masterminded and funded by foreign agents and communists, only to reconstruct public opinion in favour of American withdrawal from Vietnam which may give victory to communists on a platter. But there was no congressional enquiry on the infiltration of foreign funds and communist agents into these revolt bodies. As journalists were also following the route and policy of Congress, these charges would not be subjected to congressional enquiry, and these journalistic acts could be buried under congressional commentary.

6
No War Today In Which America Is Uninvolved

The Vietnam tragedy was not the result of a communist military victory over American forces. It was the pride of American Congress to have disabled the president by declaring war on him, and a President fated and slated to lose the war with the Congress was fated to lose the war with the enemy also. How did the American representative assembly lose its national honour is a difficult question? This is the wrong result of the doctrine of separation of powers rejected by the French (the proponents of the doctrine) as impractical; but embraced by the new democracy in America, in haste. But this power separation continues its survival in America only because America never faced a war on its territory threatening its survival. For more than two hundred years America lives oceans away from the main battle fields of the world–the First World War, the Second World War, the Korean War, the Indo-China War, The First Gulf War, the Second Gulf War etc. A disaster near her home had been the Pearl Harbour attack in 1941. The Cuban missiles Crisis never developed into a shooting war. In all these earth-quaking, earth-moving show-downs, the American territory was never really threatened. True, America after independence had faced problems on the survival of the republic and the two incidents were the English attack and the burning of the capital in 1815, and the other the civil war. English attack was merely a military expedition seeking revenge, and not an attempt to reconquer territory once they gave up. The second incident was the Civil War. There was possibility for disintegration or division of the United States during the height of Civil War, but America was a lucky nation, and so it survived it though with serious injuries. It got healed very quick, and the reconstructed state continued to grow into a more powerful political union, and then to the economic leadership of the world, and thereafter till today the American nation remains more or less uninjured. There is no American neighbour even to raise a shadow of military challenge to that country. She leads economically and technologically. Brazil once had a frightening geographical shape to challenge the United States, but it failed to grow because of rampant disorders into which it continuously ran. Canada is another case. But United States of America and Canada, being in unfailing amiability and being repositories of kindred immigrants, the politics of both remain democratically complementary. That being the basic structure of theirs, there is no suspicion that one wants to dominate the other, or to compete with the other. American-Canadian relationship is a camaraderie built on mutual trust.

It is said in a different note that some kind of turmoil is essential to keep a society dynamic and alert. Has America faced any turmoil in the 20th century? The depression of the twenties was not a dangerous emergency, as the economic power-house of America, could withstand these shocks. The strike at Pearl Harbour was never a fatal blow, because what has been lost in Pearl Harbour could be restored back immediately. The huge American military-industrial complex could produce enough munitions to replace it many times, and for the American military muscle, the strike was not a fatal blow. Has America ever lived under a threat to her existence in the 20th century? The rise of Russia as a nuclear power had changed this scene dramatically, but the American threat in response was more than a match for it. The post-war USSR or China, never possessed enough strength to threaten her as, it was too dangerous for them to attempt it. The collapse of the Soviet Union and the Warsaw Pact in 1989 changed the scene radically in favour of America once again, and once more, she could return into international isolation if she so wanted. Absence of a threat to the house of America is the main reason for the American apathy towards any outside war, and her feeling that all outside wars are only based on Americas goodwill, and not based on necessities. John Kerry-the Democratic opponent of Bush, has made a big issue of Vietnam where he was a soldier. Any American with a sense of history and self-respect, will discreetly avoid the mention of Vietnam War-the symbol of American surrender mania, incompetence, cowardice and moral collapse. But John Kerry makes it the symbol of his pride. If he was a combatant in the Vietnam war, then certainly he is the legatee of American defeat and dishonour. If elected President, what will Kerry do with Iraq? He evades to answer this question. As Goethe said, a critic is a person in whose honour there has never been raised a statue. With the philosophy of anomalous surrender and prostration as the guiding spirit, Kerry can dismantle the American leadership of the world– through, masterly evasions and policy confusions. This surrender mania and defeatism inherited from Vietnam can do one thing. He can surrender the American leadership of the world. Only in America, people are permitted to speak against the honour of the nation. But the Kerrymandering comes against the Bush policy of active containment of terror. Will Kerry continue to stand by Bush on Iraq? And after the Democratic Convention in Boston, he says 'Yes' - and after a lot of haggling.

What are the forces that compelled America to go to war in Iraq? The Great War called the First World War fought between 1914 and 1918, that consumed many great empires, is still the subject of enquires. And the causes are still being researched, rediscovered, re-invented and re-debated. Why Whilhem II of Germany went to war on the side of Austria-Hungary, to avenge the death of Arch Duke Franz Ferdinand? Were not there clear possibilities for a negotiated settlement? Why Tzar Nicholas II declared war on Germany when many of his generals cautioned him about the Russian un-preparedness in arms? Was not it possible in the early stages to stop Kaiser? If the British Foreign Secretary, Edward Gray had not withheld the ultimatum telegram to Germany for days–a telegram approved by the British Cabinet, would not have the war declaration been stopped? Or was it possible to stop the war at all, once the arrogant Wilhelm II was confident of a German Putsch and capture of Paris within fourteen days? Thus come the reasons and causes of the First World War and the ifs are never ending, and will never end also. If a world tragedy could have been averted by the mere issue of a threat by America, why America did not issue it? The reasons are American isolationism and political indecision. But there is no justification for the initial in difference if America is certainly to be pushed into the vortex of European war afterwards. America cannot do it because the Congress stands ready to oppose any move by the President. The anti-incumbent American press do not care if their lambasting of the courageous steps taken by the president later converts a comedy into an unimaginable tragedy. The tragedy of Vietnam is one example, and when the final disaster and genocide struck, it was not the media but the president who was accused of betrayal. Among the accusers of the president on this appalling humiliation, there were journalists too, and this journalistic somersault after their prolonged plea for withdrawal had been really surprising. If the American President in 1914 issued a warning to Whilhem II, the former would have been dubbed a war-monger, and hooted down by the Congress, the public and the press. That the American media have grown so powerful is an important development. Media only follows the Congress and what the Congress does, never become anti-national and anti-state, because it is part of the state. But this congressional jealousy of the presidency will only weaken the hands of the President, and that weakens the nation. At the same time, Congress does not concern if the country is humbled in international encounters. In a parliamentary democracy the leader of the house is the chief executive himself, and between the house and the prime minister there is no identity crisis. America having a parliamentary government, there would have been no difficulty in ratifying the Versailles Treaty. In the presidential system, while the Congress cannot execute the power of the government, as that job is that of the president alone, truly the Congress can execute the President, in more ways than one.

Again the question why America goes to war is not answered. Borrowing the Priestlean phrase, people go to war because war is in the great tradition. When the American Congress wants to say that it is surrender which is in the great tradition, there occurs an abysmal gap in political logic. Why people and leaders and rulers go to war? The ruler goes to war because he thinks it is a safe game in the circumstances. A world conqueror like Alexander also will not attempt to challenge an opponent evidently more powerful than he. When a war is likely to end in failure, no sensible contender goes to war, only to accept defeat. You can have a thousand justifications for going to war, but still you will not go for it when there is no prospect of victory. The great valour exemplified by the Polish people against the Russo-German invasion of 1939, and in the historic defence of Warsaw in 1944 is one case. But in 1938, Austria adopted another course, She knew well that she had no capacity to stop a German attack and so the Austrian President signed on Hitler's dotted lines, surrendered and that surrender did not look unreasonable also in that circumstance. Even when the enemy power is overwhelmingly superior, people fight, and such fight is the expression of patriotism and honour, rather than the desire for victory. But in every fight, even in stories of suicidal defences, there survives a remote hope for victory even by a heavenly chance. There is the reputation of martyrdom also. These can be the motives for a last-ditch defence of the country, but then what are the reasons that prompt an invader to conquer? Because it is convenient to do so. On Kuwait Saddam thought in that way, but he was wrong.

Conquerors do not take a high risk knowingly. War in spite of the superiority of arms and strategy, is a dangerous enterprise because at every next step, new risks come. But being dangerous itself shall not dissuade and stop a people from arms and battle. From the start of history, the pre-eminent duty of a ruler is to protect his territory and subjects from invaders. Sometimes, offence being the best form of defence, the threatened victim launches a pre-emptive strike against the invader, only to thwart the conquerors plans, the evident motive being to disorganize and disable the enemy. This is preventive war. But a democracy cannot wage a preventive war because the opposition and the daunted society will pounce upon, accusing that the government precipitated an unnecessary war on the people, and they are dying, and this is wasteful sacrifice. Thus the war diplomacy of democracy shall be different. Before going to war, the government has to wait for an armed attack, and the attack should be real and the frightened people should run in the opposite direction of the enemy advance, and then alone democracy can think of resistance at all. But still, for this unprovoked aggression, there will be political apologists who will plead for a compromise and this plea evidently developing into a justification for the naked aggression already committed. The enemy is never found fault with, and this wrong approach remains the continued disability of democracies. Unless there is a shooting war, the media and the opposition will never concede that there exists a war situation. In the United States, the role of the opposition is held by the Congress, and Congress tries its best to sabotage a war which is likely to boost the image of the President. While the Congress fights the President, the President fights the enemy and the ultimate conclusion is that with the expanding power of the Congress and the media to sabotage American wars midway, it has become almost impossible for America to fight a war and win it. The media can sabotage-the war effort by smuggling in photos on battle field anomalies and indecencies and publishing it. Betrayers are there everywhere, and they betray the national effort at war, and the Congress-media campaign really weaken the popular will to fight, and this is to enemy advantage.

Today, there is no war anywhere in which the Americans are absolutely uninvolved. In any war the predominant concern of the people is whether the war has been won. Generally there is no attempt to discover the causes of the wars fought long ago, as such attempts to enquire retrospectively are merely aimless post-mortems. But the American media and the Congress question whether there was any serious cause or grievance for America to go to war in Iraq and Afghanistan except the trigger happiness of President Bush, and his hawkish advisers. The war is fought and won already and the inclination of the media is to rob the President of any credit he may get on the stunning victory. The people of Iraq might be jubilant that they have been liberated and that is great credit for American democracy; but Congress fails its word on this great achievement. They say American soldiers are torturing prisoners, though such tortures are the silly lapses of serious wars. True evils and sins are never justified, but wars do not respect civil rights conditions, and cannot respect it also because of the murderous circumstances of war. During occupation such incidents being rare, announces only the decency of the situation. When forty million people are freed in a war of lethal arms, half-a-dozen-prisoners suffering humiliation at the hands of military is a casual error, and the President has assured the world of-bringing the guilty to book. But the attempt of American and British media is to discredit the great job of liberation through such tabloidisation. Saddam was slaughtering thousands and torturing millions and from that, hell America liberated and saved the Iraqis. Now the media allege that the torturing of American POW by Iraqi rebels and the defiling of their mutilated bodies also are because of the provocation offered by the Americans. The Congress has become tired and the media have become sick of the military success of a President, who acted boldly without caring for the admonitions of the media. Notorious that the Iraqi dictator had been a mass murder specialist. Has the American media ever said that it is the duty of the most powerful nation to liberate Iraq? No. They will not speak against a dictator, because of their unexpressed sympathies with the terrorist. The press especially the investigative journalist usually is a leftist appendage, and therefore always trying to discredit nationalism. They now attempt to sabotage the victory parade of the President.In another system of government and even in a parliamentary democracy, these media men would face prosecution but, in America they are Saddam's loyalists.

7
Stories Of Prisoner Abuse Hampering War-Effort

Some military photographs are now smuggled out of the country and sent to the press and TV, and these photographs show prisoner abuse in Iraq. This is violation of Human Rights and violation of the Geneva Convention rules on prisoners. But in Iraq , America is fighting a war and the duty of the press and non-print media is to help the war-effort and not hamper it. This war is to liberate a whole nation from terror. When America went to war in Iraq, it was a mammoth task and it wanted the support of all America. But what do the American media do? They abet and sell scandals. If there is prisoner abuse, that is a crime, and a crime is to be punished through prosecution and departmental action. If all crimes in the US are to be similarly broadcast to a wide-world audience, the image of USA will stand tarnished and indicted and the war effort sabotaged. Is it not in the best interests of the country that the war is won? Has the media no role in making the victory possible? But do they act in that way? They sell scandals and endanger national security and exult in these anti-national activities. Has the Congress no responsibility in securing victory for America in Iraq? Is there a war called the President's war and another war called the Congress war and the Congress supplying munitions and money to the Congress war only? Is the American tripartite-power-structure of separation of powers to work and defeat all presidential power-exercises? When a paranoid cannibal like Saddam is butchering thousands of his own subjects, has not the world of rule of law and human rights a duty and moral responsibility to react? True, dictators trample upon peoples rights under their foot, and they get on with it. When Pakistan butchered thousands of students in Dacca University and state terror was unleashed on East Bengalis, India intervened and liberated the land and the new state of Bangladesh was born. This intervention was clearly in breach of international law, but against the massive terror and genocide this was the only right response. What is the difference between Indian intervention in East Pakistan and the Americas intervention in Iraq? The day when we considered it a pure and simple domestic problem is over, and such crimes against humanity make a rightful realm for international intervention.

People fight a liberation war and the fighters sacrifice their lives in order to make the life of millions of unfree free, and this is the history of liberation wars. Some people fight liberation wars with the help of foreign powers and some fight it them-selves. Now there is no liberation war unaided by a foreign power. Some liberation wars are fought on behalf of the client people, and one example is India liberating East Pakistan in 1971, America liberating Kuwait from Iraq in 1991, Zambia liberating Uganda from Idi Amin etc. Now the Iraqi people are being liberated by America and Britain from that murderous dictator Saddam Hussein, and that liberation will be complete only with restoration of law and order and the establishment of an organised government. If in the turmoil created by some bomb blasts by terrorists, America is leaving Iraq abandoning it to the strangle hold of another dictator—(and the population of possible dictators in the Middle East being very high)—then the two Gulf Wars were fought in vain. America remaining in Iraq till the gains of war are consolidated and organised into new self-government, must be in the best interests of that country. It shall not be forgotten that the American people applauded George Bush as a great liberator when he overthrew Saddam Hussein, with a vengeance.

The media always work against an active and strong president and the main weapon of the media is scandal. Prisoner abuse is a scandal. The Iraqi people constantly slapped with the outrageous prison practices of Saddam will not be and need not be surprised of the minor prisoner abuse by US soldiers. The whole-sale indignation comes from US media men and the Bush enemies who want to invent crimes to sabotage a Bush re-election in November 2004. Concerted and massive effort are being made by the media to damage the Bush candidacy by highlighting on his errors, and blacking out the spectacular success areas of Iraqi liberation. It has become an endemic disease of the American media to damage and destabilises the executive and thwart great projects Nixon was hand-cuffed by Watergate. Against the lack-lustre, do nothing Ford and Carter, the media had no enmity but only sympathy. Against the strong presidency of Ronald Reagan, there was the Iran-contra, but Reagan fought it out and survived, and at last after a decade long enquiry by the special counsel Lawrence Walsh, the case fizzled out. Then came Bush Sr. who fought and won the war and then surrendered and so the media had only sympathy for him. But being a strong intervener in the beginning, they were raising all objections under international law against Bush Sr. also. The Clinton legacy is really fantastic. A besieged government of misconduct from corruption to philandering to womanising. But it was an age of economic prosperity. Always the president was under the shadow of the Independent Counsel-Kenneth Starr. Starr was investigating the White Water Corporation case and then the earth-shaker, crime thriller the Monica Lewinsky story. The impeachment juggernaut was set in motion and it took its toll on the administration. But it is the people of the United States who fought and vanquished the predatory media, the Congress and the pornographer-Kenneth Starr. People proclaimed that a sexual favour from an unmarried woman is not a ground to impeach the President and they condemned its proponents. The senate, fearing a massive backlash from the public dismissed the impeachment motion presented by the House. When compared with the Nixon guilt reconstructed on multiple untruth in the Watergate, there was proved misconduct on the part of Clinton but the trigger-happy senators had to undergo a shameful withdrawal in the end.Clinton was acquitted in spite of misconduct, as there were not the required votes in the senate. But against Nixon there were the necessary Senate votes in spite of his guilt being manipulated and overblown by enemies. Now impeachment is on the basis of votes and not on the basis of guilt built on high crimes. High time that the scandal-mongers are brought to justice and the dynamism of the administration restored. If one American soldier, on his voluntary choice is abusing a prisoner in Iraq, that small incident in magnified into an international crime against humanity and the, President is sought to be tried on this crime committed by a petty-soldier, oceans away. Do not the media know that the leadership of the President is to be preserved and protected not only for the protection of America, but for the protection of the free world? But the Congress is never concerned that America must win a war she started; on the contrary they do all in their power to ensure the defeat of any American war including the Korean War, the Vietnam war, the Iraq War etc. The stand of the Congress is as bad as anti-state because they plead and act for the defeat of the United States. The same treasonable stand is followed by the media and they are protected from this offence only because they follow the congressional path. Because of the notorious anti-President stand of the Congress, the crime of the media is euphemized as political criticism and the nation suffers. Has the media ever pleaded that the forty million Iraqis are groaning under Saddam terror, and the United States, as democracy's policeman, shall intervene? No, they have no such mission for the rights of man. If forty millions are liberated into freedom is it no important event on the rights of man! But when five prisoners are abused, that incident is advertised to the whole world audience misinforming them that Americans in Iraq are engaged in crimes against humanity. They simply want to tarnish and thereby disable the presidency and this is nothing but an anti-liberation act. But American democracy treats them as heroes.

When the media turns inimical with the scandal weapon in its armoury, they cite popularity ratings as the measuring rod of presidential power. A President is elected for 4 years, and that mandate runs for the whole period unless he is impeached. What is the meaning and need of ascertaining the daily popularity ratings of the President? Is the President to be re-elected every morning? Why a President or Prime Minister is elected to rule and take that power on behalf of the people? A mob cannot rule and the mob cannot be wise and statesmanly, and it cannot be disciplined, assertive and it cannot lead. Why the Congress is not given executive power? Because Congress is a crowd of hundreds and a pandemonium of hundreds cannot take administrative decisions quickly, the decisive quickness of a decision being very important in governance. The ruler shall be courageous to take un-popular decisions, when un-popular decisions alone are safe and needed. See the time of war–If a country is going to be attacked by the enemy and the signals are clear, it will be wiser for the defending country to go on the offensive and make a preventive strike. But when a preventive strike is to be made, it will be a very unpopular measure as a fearful people misinformed and misguided by a cowardly opposition are most likely to oppose the preventive strike and, say that the President is precipitating a dangerous crisis and inviting a war. But in truth it will be a military strike that would prevent a more costly and deadly war. States derive power through by different systems by autocracy, by monarchy, oligarchy, dictatorship, totalitarianism, military rule, limited democracy, full democracy etc. But popularity exercises occur only in democracies and fortunately the leading governments in the world today like the United States, United Kingdom, Japan, Germany, France, Italy, India, Turkey, Canada, Mexico, Australia, Philippines, South Africa and perhaps Russia are democracies and it is to the credit of humanity that the non-democratic world is shrinking. Let us again come to the question of the daily popularity ratings reconstructed by the news media. In their feverish search to sell news, often they create and manufacture news to fill headlines, and as an institutional art they invent every kind of news. A new addition has been the gallop-poll which was founded to predict American President elections and Congress elections. Some times it came close to truth and sometimes close to falsity and therefore getting the bad name of manipulation made to help a particular political party. It was during the 1948–Truman-

Tom Dewey contest that Gallop who predicated a massive win for Dewey came to grief. Those who voted believing the prediction felt deceived. Still Gallop poll continues, of course with lesser fascination and failing credibility with many new competitors. Exit polls and poll surveys are simply gambles, but during election time its entertainment value is truly high.

The sample polls branched off into opinion survey and exit poll-which are new specialist advances. These predications claim a scientific basis or an empirical basis, but of late it degenerated into party survey and propaganda. The pollsters predict popularity one day and drops the other day. Whether the common man is the best judge of the complicated, intricate daily or hourly policy moves of the ruler, is an important question. The governed alone can know whether the President is a success in foreign policy; whether he is a failure in the economic front, whether the security of the country is safe in his hands, whether the war fought by the country is won or lost etc. But can the common man assess and evaluate the daily moves in administrative minutiae? The pollster comes to contend that the common man is a statesman and therefore capable of evaluating a ruler on the basis of his shortest administrative intervals of hourly or daily. In this assumption by the media when the pollster is correct, then even a mob can rule the country. The City States of Greece were ruled by the assembly comprising the whole population, but those states, though the cultural and knowledge store-houses of the world, collapsed when bigger states invaded them. The argument that the common man can give daily advice to the ruler is a media fiction unscientific and an erroneous reading of political history. Then why do pollsters publish the daily or weekly ratings? When a war is in progress, the army may be on the forward move in the morning but making a tactical retreat in the evening, and if this is informed to the public, the rating will be high in the morning and low in the evening. Is there a more incorrect assessment of the ruler? Then the question is why the pollsters are delving in this unseemly trade. Because this is big media business, and they don't care if this project is an unethical exploitation of reader sensibilities. The American media now publish that the President is unpopular in the morning, and he has to attain popularity in the evening, if he has to retain the right to remain in Oval Office. What is the legal, political and moral basis of this media claim? Do the political theory of democracy say that the President has to seek the consent of the electorate every morning? A Statesman is to be judged on the basis of all his plus and minus points in his whole tenure, and not on the basis of his hourly popularities including the times he sleep.

Wars become necessary, and wars are often an inevitable necessity because even on a peaceful country war can be imposed by a belligerent nation. But put this question of war for a popular referendum. The enemies of war will immediately join hands with the alien invader and propagate against going to war. The basic reason is that war, being as unpleasant as dangerous, the common man–a lover of pleasure and irresponsibility–will vote for peace and not for war. He does not care if such peace is merely surrender, because he is not informed of the lessons of patriotism and the honour of success and the necessity for territorial security. His gluttonous persuasions are allowed a free run.

Bush is vilified that the Iraqi prisoners of war are abused by the American army. In war also, revenge and retaliations are possible things, which are wrong but natural, and it is only some weeks before these abuse episode was brought before world audience that three

American business contractors were killed and dragged through the streets, by Iraqi rebels. There were protests by coalition governments, but no serious protest by media. Perhaps the media think that the American businessmen do deserve it as the bearers of American sin. There were only feeble comments that the prisoner abuse is the result of the cruelty shown on the American captives by the Iraqi terrorists. These terrorists are paid by fundamentalists to carry out murderous explosions throughout the free world, where the print and electronic media hide their crimes. Very sorry the innuendos, arguments and researches and investigative discoveries of the media tend only to injure the pride and honour of the democratic system, of which the media-man is the primary by-product. However, the mediamen in USA, and now in Britain follows the anti-national route, and damage the interest of his own country. A foreigner cannot sabotage another country, because being a foreigner, he can only wage a war against the alien country. Here the media are waging war against their own country–the USA, and patriotism stands on its legs.

In war and love, anything is fair and this is historic. The inclination of the American media is to declare that war is a bad thing, a kind of political sport to kill innocent people. Not yet there is a war in the world that does not kill warriors but modern technology has reduced the death rate drastically. The more the technological superiority of the attacker, the less the number of casualties on their side. But remember, technology has multiplied the casualities of the opponent in case the opponent's war machine is technologically inferior. This happened in Iraq. In the Iraq war, the number of Coalition dead were counted as less than 150, whereas, the Iraqis suffered a casuality of more than 10,000. But in spite of this tremendous advantage secured by the Anglo-American forces, the western media, especially the prowling electronic media accuse Bush of unnecessary American casualities. Is there any country in the world including Western democracies who complain that soldiers are dying in the war and therefore the government in power is guilty? The motive of American media is in misinforming the gullible public. How many hundred thousands died in the American Civil War? It is more than half a million. How many died in the First World War and in the Second World War? Was there any accusation that soldiers, due to poor generalling were sacrificed as cannon-fodder and such sacrifices should have been avoided? Commanding a war is a very high art and craft. A great general sacrifices a lesser number than an ordinary general, but policy decisions shall not be questioned. If a general is to be taken to task in this way, then he will be hesitating to take risky decisions and such hesitation is the greatest danger for war. Can Congress suggest a strategy which wins the war, but does not kill soldiers? Can the print or electronic-media suggest a strategy that wins a war without killing soldiers? The most unpatriotic and irresponsible criticism this has been. What is the interest of the nation they simply ignore as irrelevant in the war-dialogue. They want to criticise, and they are fond of scandals only.

8
Is The War Won Or Lost?

On 07-04-2004 the United States Congress summoned the Defence Secretary Rumsfeld for testimony on the allegations of prisoner abuse by American soldiers in Iraq. Such an interrogation by Congressmen, and what will be its ultimate effect on the prosecution of war? In 1999, India went to war with Pakistan on the Kargill incursions, and India won the battle repelling the intruders. This writer attended a seminar convened by journalists and intellectuals. The seminarists agreed that the battle has been won by India, but the leftist critics were more concerned about the propriety of the language used by the defence minister and they tend to think that victory was something the nation did not need. When the war was won, the media stand concerned with the linguistic merits of the defence ministers press note, but unconcerned of the victory accomplished at great cost and sacrifice. Many speakers were leftists and therefore uncaring of territorial nationalism, war and victory. These critics raise their anti-state arguments under different garbs and masks, but essentially their stand is anti-state. The prejudiced American Congress is unwilling to admit that the President has liberated Iraq and won a stunning victory against Saddam–the tyrant and criminal—against humanity.

A syndicate of the Congress and the media is a very powerful competent combination, and can attack capable executives and strong governance. The media seems to maintain a vested interest in weakening a strong ruler, but forgetting the fact that such postures weaken the war efforts and the final beneficiaries of such acts are the enemies of the United States. When the media launched Watergate, the direct beneficiary was world communism, North Vietnam and China. When Bush and Rumsfeld are found fault with, the beneficiaries are Bin Laden, Saddam Hussein and terrorists. The media will swear that they are for the liberation of Iraq; but they will do only things which not only encourage and promote terrorism, but aid it also. It is due to such dangers inherent in the war effort that states have enacted and decreed the law that anything aiding the enemy during war is treason. But now what do they do? During war they plead for the enemy and support their cause under the cover of strange political philosophies only to cause the defeat of national forces. A beleaguered President—George W. Bush has to submit to these treasonable onslaughts because he has to face re-election which is only weeks away. So he suffers all these arguments by the media abetting the Congress to the role of a conspirator. Congress has only one vested interest and that is the defeat and humiliation of the President. Unconcerned they are if the American war in Iraq ends in the defeat of the United States and Iraqis going back to the Saddam terror after expelling the Coalition forces. That this Congress-President rivalry is the direct result of separation of powers is no overstatement. The framers should have made America a parliamentary democracy with an independent judiciary invested which the power of judicial review as done in India. Only due to the egotism of leaders in congressional caucuses, the Congressmen argued for rejecting the Versailles Treaty and the Senate followed suit and this turned out the most wretched decision in the century. So the blood of millions of martyrs shed on the plains and marshes of Europe during 1914-18 was in vain, and once again the clouds of war gathered over Europe and the world; and within twenty years, the world was ready for another tragedy. All reasons point to the conclusion that the Second World War was the direct result of American refusal to ratify the Versailles Treaty. American President Wilson framed the Treaty but left it in Europe as an international orphan, and Hitler came to tear it down causing the catastrophe of Second World War.

The attempt of the Congress is to see the President defeated in the next poll on the basis of the misinformation collected and supplied from the battle scenes in Iraq. When the Vietnam war was lost, the American Congress was celebrating it and when the Versailles Treaty was thrown out the Congress was jubilant. Is separation of powers creating different and opposing loyalties for different departments of the state? The American military says that the prisoners were being interrogated to collect information on the Saddam regime. If a prisoner is questioned as a witness under civil procedure in a court of law, how much true information will such prisoner speak to the enemy? If the American government wants to get real information on high secrets, uncivil methods are to be employed, and this will be in violation of the Geneva Convention. Questioning the Iraqi prisoners under civil rules will be as bad as seeking the consent of the Iraqi people for bombing them. How are these military photos which are top secret military documents leaked out and smuggled to the press, is a very important security lapse to investigate. To impede the American war effort, there are informers, spies and enemies infiltrating and operating the military system.

Not to mention the patriotism of the news agencies who telecast these secret documents before being declassified by authorities. How can the American Congress celebrate this national insult? If there is an investigation, that is to be done after the war. Congress may look in retrospect that the nonratification of the Versailles Treaty and her consequent non joining of the League of Nations—the main offspring begotten at Versailles, places the entire guilt for the un-stoppable arms race following it, squarely on the Congress of the United States. And for this guilt history is showering curses on that Capitoline syndicate. The sins of the Vietnam disaster is pointing its accusation on the anti-Nixon tirades of the congressional fearfuls who usually tremble on hearing the word 'war'. In another country these congressional obstructers would have been prosecuted, condemned and punished; but in America they go scotch free. See the wonders that separation of power is blowing up! Separation of powers is really a brake on the car going uphill. It harbours Trojan Horses under the cover of right to information. Can misinformation reach more absurd, dangerous heights?

In1947, the year of Indian Independence, Dubya was born to George Bush Sr, who was then building up his oil business in Texas. Molly Irvins gives a rash account of the happy life of George W. Bush-the President of USA since January 2001, and now slated for a tough re-election in November 2004. We read through the happy life of Bush Jr. who was smoking marijuana, and escaping unpunished because of his important father who was congressman, CIA Chief, Vice-President and then President, presiding over the First Iraq War. That war did liberate Iraq but resold again to Saddam. On restoration, Saddam could identify those irrepressible freedom lovers who wrongly believed that on the military triumph of America the Saddam terror is finally over. But what followed in Iraq on resale was the vengeful ferocity of the dictator for retaliation against his enemies. Followed the great terror and purge once again that bled the country to moribund submission once again. This was the result of the irresolute and wavering-policy of Sr. Bush and his commander Collin Powell, now presiding over the state department. That great liberation war and its results were flowed down Euphrates and Tigris and a humiliated America punished Bush Sr, by the resounding rejection of his re-election bid in 1992. Bush Sr. is the President who surrendered after winning the war, and this uncommon military logic was rejected by American people. The thousands of Iraqis, who believing in their final release from Saddam bondage, revolted and exulted in the victory parade could find themselves sold out, and these thousands were caught as traitors and butchered by Saddam. This was a sin committed by Bush Sr. because of wavering irresolution, and defeatist pacifism, and this is a sin which must be atoned if time gives the chance. Jr. Bush must have been resentful of his father's decision in 1991 and desired to unmake the surrender executed against the will of America. George W. Bush looks determined to bring back American honour, but to do that he must become the President of the United States. Will he be? But 2000 November sprang another surprise and Bush Jr. is the President of the United States through a minority vote. This is an electoral accident in the time-tested American democratic process.

George W. Bush studied law-and holds an MBA from Harward but being unfascinated by the profession he never put on the robes of a lawyer. He hates reading long books and essays and thinks great scholarship is the unwanted burden of a statesman. Reading long, laborious reports of commissions of enquiry or expert panels, never he attends to. He believes that statesmanly actions need not be scholarly actions, and history tells a German story. To ridicule the style of governance of Edward Gladstone, his contemporary Otto Von Bismarck called him professor. It is good that the President should have an intimate knowledge of the nation, people and problems. And desirable if he knows something more about their history and religion, but unnecessary that he should be a scholar on political science.

Bush, though unscholarly, is an effective speaker and seldom he sojurns into wilderness. He does not avoid direct answers as he hates circumlocution. He is emphatic on his policies and does not engage in the game of vacillation. He defends his subordinates with sincerity and does not throw them to political wolves. This conduct sharply contrasts with the, conduct of Richard Nixon-who in the desperation of the Watergate siege, sacrified his ardent supporters and long-time associates like Haldeman-Erlichman etc. and found himself deserted by sincere associates in the White House in his last days in Washington. He had to accept a chief of staff, like Alexander Haig who speeded up the demolition process of his presidency. It was the Haig selection of Jaworski which culminated in the demand for tapes that led to the Nixon resignation. But Bush acts differently. Rumsfeld, the Defence Secretary has been grilled by Congress on the question of prisoner abuse and as usual, being a scandalous issue in American democracy, the President facing a re-election also, should speak on it. As damage control, another President would have thought is wiser to cashier in his defence Secretary as a scape-goat, and wash his hands. But that would be a bad legacy for a statesman, and a very wrong signal to his future defenders. A courageous defender is not disowned by the United States President. Defence Secretary Rumsfeld is a very tough and effective leader of Afghan and Iraqi invasions. Once he was rising star in the Republican Party and an opponent of Sr. Bush. He on Iraq instructed and encouraged the President to go it alone also if necessary. These prisoner abuses may not be on the orders of the defence secretary, but being military's operational inside story, it is his duty to take action, but keep it away from public view, as it will affect military morale and war-efforts. As a matter of policy strategy, and confidence building, sometimes action against the military will have to be postponed, if it affects the American activities in Iraq. But betrayers are there, and it is the informers in the army itself who leaked the pictures to the media, who are eager to grab any chance to beat a strong President. This by the media is an anti-national step in practice, but pictured as a patriotic act. When the American contractors were abducted, killed, mutilated and dragged through the streets, the American media had no grief, and they did not call for revenge. When such cruelty is committed by the enemy, is it not natural that there will be desire for revenge? The highest point of human rights violation is killing a human being. But there is no complaint by the media that unnecessary killings and fake-encounters are taking place in Iraq. Their complaint is that a prisoner has been humiliated, whereas terrorists mutilate their victims. The Iraqi terrorist will mutilate the bodies of Americans and drag them through streets, but America should treat the POW with extreme decency as shown in democratic civil societies - a very good ideal to preach, but very difficult to practice in an atmosphere of revengeful emotional upsurge and martial high-handedness. It is now revealed that America failed to pre-establish an organisation to administer Iraq, after a quick war. But in every war, the capacity to reestablish law and order differs from government to government and in any case this needs a substantial increase in troop deployment and introduction of para-military forces. It is natural to expect that the anti-socials and terrorists will badly exploit the disorder arising out of a Saddam collapse all on a sudden; There occurred massive lootings including the looting of the world famous artefacts in the Baghdad Museum. The regrettable part is that violence and looting became so massive and easy for the under-world to commit that it became difficult later on to control and restore law and order.

9
Japan, Germany, Marshall Plan And Reconstruction

The world is attempting to compare the history of re-construction of Japan and Western Europe after the Second World War, but the Anglo-American efforts in Iraq and Afghanistan are challenged and sabotaged by terrorist resistance. Iraqis think that the Anglo-American re-construction of Iraq is the second line of invasion, and it is a concrete attempt at re-colonisation of a country, which was decolonised by the English after the Second World War. There is not even an unorganised democratic movement in Iraq and the Baathist Party is now a religious as well as political terror-outfit of Saddam, who will never compromise with the philosophy of re-construction and political orderliness. The Iraqi stand is to push out the coalition at the earliest and deny any credit to the invaders for doing good things to the Iraqi people. Imagine the people of Germany and Japan conducting a guerrilla war against the Marshall Plan, and the Mc-Arthur Plan. Then the presently prosperous, powerful countries like Japan and Germany would not have been reborn. Some dictator would have been ruling these countries now and the countries once more plunging into civil war and disintegration. But the people were disciplined and they acted wisely and patriotically and they found no evil motives behind the American move for massive aid and reconstruction. Conflict gave way to cooperation, and cooperation opened the era for the largest reconstruction project in history – the Marshall Plan. Within five years. Germany, Western Europe and Japan were back on their legs. The most important achievement is that these countries, under the protection of their own growing wealth could resist the overtures and strangle-hold of communist totalitarianism which was making imperial in-roads of ideology into the liberated areas. With American co-operation and aid, Japan and Germany are again the economic power-houses of Europe and Asia. These two examples are sufficient to guide Iraqis to the reality that if they cooperate with the occupation powers, she being oil rich, can race into a well-developed nation–a nation with technological excellence also. But then Iraqi rebels are fascinated neither by the prospect of a high velocity growth and prosperity coming out of democratic governance. In spite of these guerrilla bombings, considerable headway has already been made by coalition forces, and now Iraqis are getting food, clothing and medicine they want. If they want to grow rich this is the splendid occasion, but middle easterners think narrowly.

As the history of the Middle East goes, they want to live in the terrorist game of bomb-blasts, and innocents killings. They cannot imagine that they are under American occupation, and they refuse to accept that truth. Even after a most humiliating defeat, they are refusing to admit they have lost the war and they are under occupation. Against this day-light reality, what is the use of these denials? The Japanese, the most virulent invaders in the Second World War, quickly changed track and, accepted American aid and advice.They believed in the American promise to return the land back to them. Quite unusual that it was the man in uniform Mc Arthur who gave a democratic constitution to Japan under the auspices of which Japan renounced war and raced into prosperity. This was exactly what Western Europe, including Germany also did, and they accepted the Marshall Plan and speeded towards rapid economic growth. If Western Europe also refused American aid, treating it as against their national interest and self-respect, the economic miseries of war would have been persecuting Europe and Japan far longer, and the sufferings of the people would have been reaching distressing shapes. Without sufficient United States aid, the German and Japanese Economic miracles would never have become an immediate reality.

Like an entrepreneur trying to borrow credit to build his factory; a nation in distress, if they want prosperity, must raise credit and other means of production and the universal practice has been to borrow from rich countries. May be that America was having the motive to help the countries in need, and Soviet Union in her powerful days had established her own funding agencies to help the needy especially the ideologically like-minded. Aids are in different ways, like money loans, grants, soft loans project grants etc. There is also technology transfer and transfer of expertise and technicians. Western Europe and Japan whole-heartedly and eagerly accepted American aid as a boon, and, they treated the occupier as friend and patron, and America on her part kept her promises. These countries renounced their militarism and made no hesitation to accept democracy as future form of government. It was a negotiated embrace between the conqueror and the conquered, and these countries marched into the reconstruction work of the nation. What followed was a dazzling performance which patron America would rather envy at. The only prejudice these underdogs suffered was disarmament, but they wanted its conscientiously and the Japanese draftsmen of the Mc. Arthur constitution too were willing to include a clause in the Constitution renouncing re-arming permanently. American occupation of Philippines is another instance of occupation followed by liberation and that country continues an American ally today. True, times have changed and France, Germany, Japan etc. under-went peaceful economic revolutions and these changes include policy changes into anti–Americanism It is not only the American presidents-but it is the American democracy, its human rights debates, the caucuses in the Congress and the media that set the tone for American wars of occupation and liberation. American occupation of Western Europe and Japan, in fact led not only to de-occupation, but to the liberation from Fascist and Nazit dictatorships.But those great arguments which mesmerized millions in Italy and Germany no more fascinate them once they came under the spell of full freedom. These examples of American authored liberation, re-construction and resurgence are true examples of the decolonised free, and the prospective free, but this could not be driven home to Iraqi fundamentalists and Saddam loyalists. At the same time, these loyalists are not a big number to look a democratic crowd, also. They are only a small number, but they are all equipped with bombs, the ideology of bombing, and the large number of martyrs they produce. Before the Second World War, the Muslim fundamentalists were not terrorists but only religious fanatics. But the new prosperity donated by petro-dollars built up a new generation of wealthy terrorists whose sacrifices and martyrdom are well compensated by money payments and rich family supports. Terrorist include today suicide bombers and those suicides are never more deterred by the prospect of their families going orphaned in the extreme sacrifice they commit in the terror game. Once they are ready to commit their life, they are assured that their families are wholly taken care of, and well supported. The martyrdom of the terrorist brings in not only wealth but religious halo around their soul.

The most pertinent question is whether these terror machines are really looking for the liberation of people being held under colonial servitude, oppression and captivity. One cannot deny the truth that America and Britain are in occupation of Iraq. In the face of that reality the question is what options are to be given to the Americans before leaving Iraq. Once Americans are speeding up to draw the road-map and schedule for their packing out, the first essential of the new Iraqi regime is to establish law and order, and hand over effective control to civil authority representing the different tribal loyalties, and then conduct a free and fair poll to elect a democratic government, representative of the people.But a democratically elected popular government is the nightmare of all fundamentalist regimes and organizations in the petro-dollar-rich Middle East. There is no democracy in the Middle East except in Israel. Lebanon is occasionally and partly democratic, Turkey is an almost democracy and Syria is a one-party dictatorship where a dynasty is being founded. Egypt is a quasi-dictatorship where also a dynasty is in the making. Kuwait is monarchy; Iraq had been a dictatorship-but now democratizing under Anglo-American care. Iran, claiming to be a pseudo-democracy is living under the spell of religious fundamentalism and therefore unpredictable. Saudi Arabia is a monarchy. United Arab Emirates are princedoms; Libya is a dictatorship, Algeria after a long spell under dictatorship, is limping back into doubtful democracy and Morocco is a monarchy. Of these Libya, Algeria and Morocco are not necessarily Middle East countries, but they too are Muslim states in very near neighbourhood. When America wants to establish democracy in Iraq, the whole Middle East region is going in turmoil and shock, and they fear their own systems being threatened with the coming democratic disorder. Not improbable that the most faithful US ally in the area-Saudi Arabia herself will finance a project to scuttle the American experiment in Iraqi democractisation, and their immediate choice will be to seek the help of terrorists. It is well known that the master terrorist Osama Bin Laden–the genius behind September/11, is a Saudi Prince, and his wealth provides the main stay for his global terror-machine. When America dreams of an Iraqi democratic revolution, is there is a single neighbour (Israel cannot take part in the argument) who really supports it? There is none, and most of them shudder at the thought of a neighbour harbouring true democracy. As a free country can be a real threat to their own system and existence, there is no surprise that American schemes are sought to be engulfed in terror bombings, If financial support for these counter-measures come from the Arabian comrades of America themselves, it is only a natural.

The Saddam supporters must have different causes to oppose and defeat American proposals. True against the call for liberation and a free democracy, there cannot be a moral argument, and so the terrorists seldom come forward with arguments, but they call for Jihad. In another country, a liberation war is very difficult to stop, except through bloody suppression as it happened in Tiananmen Square in Peking in 1989. But in the Muslim countries in the Middle East, freedom will be opposed as licentious disorder. This is on theocratic disapproval, and therefore the terror bombings have become almost a way of Islamic freedom of expression. Democrats will blame this posture as a political danger to people's rights, but this dangerousness is not the concern of the religions fanatic and the fundamentalist.

10
America Liberates And That In Certain Promise

The stand taken by the free world in liberation and decolonisation is as bewildering as a self contradiction. The print media and the electronic media are now ruling the skies, the eye, the ear and soul of man. It is the media who shall come forward to defend wars of liberation, and human rights. The American War of Independence was a war against Britain, but that war was encouraged and abetted by the French, short of armed intervention in favour of the insurrectionists. May be the French authorities were jealous of the British empire having such large continents as colonies, and out of political ill will alone they might have aided the American War of Independence. When democracy is on the upsurge, and all leading powers of the world except China are democrats, there is overwhelming moral justification for the spread and founding of democracy throughout the world, and this democratisation should remain the main battle of the freeman. What is America doing in Iraq? The world media vehemently plead for the expulsion of American forces, as what America does is not liberation, but enslavement of a nation. The most dastardly, murderous regime in the post-war world is patronised by the media, and they give no straight answers to these questions. If some terrorist with evident democratic leanings is bombing and killing innocent people, that is pictured by the media as a liberation war. In the freedom struggle of India, there were terrorists, extremists as well as moderate revolters, but none thinking of a strategy of going to the undefended villages and killing unarmed poor farmers to frighten British authorities. Such a move by any nationalist would have made him anti-Indian, anti-people and traitorous in the eyes of the nationalist Indian revolters. If they employed terror, employed it directly against the British, their supporters and informers. But here is a new strategy invented by red-guerillas, especially in the Indo-China jungles. The effectiveness of this strategy of mass-killing through terrorist bombings of innocents was first practiced by the red guerillas there–who had no intention of liberating people to democracy. They wanted the foreign power–the French as 'colony-owner' to leave. Also they wanted Americans as defenders of the South Vietnam (from 1954 to 1975) to leave South Vietnam and prepare the territory for a naked take-over by the North. It was not war, but terrorism and massacres to enslave the people, but, such enslavement has been pictured by the media as liberation (If these people are not subjected to totalitarian regimentation later on, that was only due to liberalisation of the terror-machine, and also due to political compulsions and the fall of communism world over). The breach of Geneva Agreement, the naked aggression and occupation of South Vietnam due to the disastrous withdrawal executed by a defeatist Gerald Ford, the more than one million South Vietnamese who died drowning in the South China sea or in the inhuman slaughter by the Vietcong are flattered into liberation wars by the media, but in fact these were genocides. Indo-China-including Vietnam, Laos and Cambodia were French colonies once, and in the war of liberation, Ho–

Chi-Minh won a great victory at Dien Bien Phu and the French colonists were forced to leave in humiliation and grief. In the 1954 Geneva agreement, Vietnam was divided into two–North and South and the North was given to Ho Chi Minh and the South to Ngo Din Diem. The North established a totalitarian State and the South an authoritarian democracy. This partition was on the conditions of an agreement reached at Geneva, and this Treaty of 1954 ought to be the permanent document making two Vietnams. But North wanted to take over the South also, and in naked breach of the Geneva Agreement, they unleashed a war of terror against the south and the south asked for American help, and help had to come in a very big way and it came. In the height of war Denang became the biggest naval base in the world and at the peak of combat the American soldiers numbered more than half a million. Of these above fifty five thousand died in the war. But the fundamental American flaw was that they never attempted to invade the North. They defended and defended without offending, and the United States troops never crossed the ceasefire line of 1954. American media lashed out against President Johnson who committed a large troop contigent, but he never gave the order to invade the North. Then came Nixon whose election promise was withdrawal from Vietnam the most encouraging news for the victorious guerillas. But Nixon had an untimely exit because of Watergate and Watergate did great help for America's enemies. Had Nixon continued in office, he, being resourceful, courageous and daring would not have allowed Vietnam to go down the drain. But the irresolute Ford and the shuttle man-Henry Kissinger executed there the most meekly surrender in history. American surrender was the surrender of the freedom of the people of South Vietnam. After the most expensive, excruciating and bloody war, how America, commanded by a defeatist Congress, and abetted by the media surrendered, remains a great puzzle. But the American Congress and the media celebrated this surrender as a great occasion for rejoicing. The liberated are the five hundred thousand American troops and that was the reason for congressional rejoicing. The people they went to defend and save are mercilessly thrown into the machine of red-terror. This is the kind of liberation which the perverted vision of the media advocated. Quite willingly the Congress follows the media and the media is perpetually at war with the President. If the executive want to execute strong policies the media intervenes and the cold war suddenly develops into a shooting war, the media firing the first salvo and this salvo will be in the form of a scandal. Some scandals click and others die out, but before one dies, many more are invented and re-launched and this disabling game continues.

The surrender in Vietnam remains one of the self imposed tragedies of America. When wars are raging it is to America that the world looks for guidance, leadership and help. This was the case in the two World Wars and more so in the post-War World. So is the case of, Korea, Greece, Italy, Vietnam, Latin America, etc. There are many small Latin American countries like Panama, Guatemala, Nicaragua, Cuba and Dominican Republic-where America regularly intervened under a geographical privilege. In Korea, America almost succeeded in recapturing the conquered South and in re-establishing it as a powerful economic entity of the east. In Taiwan a Chinese take over has been foiled by successive American administrations, but on Vietnam it is a different story. Perhaps the campus bombings and the media campaign against American intervention destroyed the fabric of American morality in foreign policy, and in this confrontation, the congressional hostility to the Presidency reached murderous levels. Sometimes it looked even a congressional conspiracy with the enemy to defeat the United States. Congress passed the War Power Act, which placed the American soldier in the battlefield in chains. Important to remember the words of George Washington in the Philadelphia Convention. A majority of delegates were concerned that a powerful executive–a single man President–may turn into a dictator or monarch, and in order to permanently check this sabotage, they suggested an article in the Constitution limiting the standing army of the new United States to five thousand troops. Washington responded saying that one more clause be added directing all foreign countries not to attack United States with more than five thousand troops. This answer contains the argument on the futility of the proposal. The humour and good sense of those delegates are not in the possession of present day congressmen, and they indulge in anti-American activities, under the mask of separation of powers. America remains the leader of the world not because of the Congress but in spite of they and she remains an open society not because of her free press but in spite of they. The background of media activities like any other aspect of human life should be accessible to the public for scrutiny, and it should be transparent for the people to see. But will they allow even to peep into the secrecies and conspiracies existing as background to every news item and scandal they launch into the audience of the credulous? The media plays the game of sabotage of national honour and that honour is being surrendered to the enemy. When the executive disobeys their commands they do the scandals bombings, and scandal are the terror-bombings of the media.The confusion of interdepartmental rivalry generated a free for all political situation under separation of powers and that scuttled American victories in many theatres of conflict and such reversals only helping the growth of Communism world wide. But Communism still collapsed not because of America, but in spite of American imbecility and weakness. The question is when do the American Congress and the press realise the true importance and need of the power of the executive to lead in world affairs?

Fortunately for Bush, there is no indication that directions came directly from the Oval Office to Baghdad to abuse the prisoners of war. After the war and capture, there was lack of coordination in military organisation, and so discipline was lax as the Iraqi resistance crumbled in no time and success came so unexpectedly to accommodate in full. Regarding the timing of the conclusion of battles, no contender is able to foresee and make advance arrangements for changes into civil order. The latest reports say that shortage of security staff affected prison discipline and in certain places even one third of the required staff was not available and this security lapse, unnoticed by the military leadership, was leading to indiscipline and abuses.

But immediately after the end of combat and the acceptance of surrender, the first priority of the occupier (here the coalition) is return to civil rule and withdraw martial law at the earliest. Along with restoration of law and order, there is the big task of restoring the minimum infrastructure for the return of normalcy, or rather the reestablishment of normalcy. Truly much of the work to restore infrastructure to supply food and cloths to the population is already over. However, what do the media do? After the war the media are attempting to dig out only scandals and they suppress all the good work done by the occupation forces. The British Foreign

Secretary claims that tremendous progress has been made in the field of reconstruction, but these good aspects are deliberately sidelined and ignored by the media. Viewed in this context, it is clear that the media are hunting for scandals only too jeopardize the war and reconstruction work and this is clearly helping the enemy. When the coalition forces are caught in the smear campaign, it results in the unpopularity of coalition government and in the debate of democracies, the enemy becomes more powerful to stall the reconstruction programme.

We see the present state of Palestine where the Gaza Strip is always in revolt. There are attacks and counter attacks and the Israeli armed superiority and determination are under challenge. There were hundreds of negotiations for a settlement of the Palestine question but the Palestine leadership has no plan for peace and it looks they want to keep this question alive for ever. After the Six Day War in 1967, almost all the territory occupied by Israel have been returned during the shuttle diplomacy of Henry Kissinger and afterwards. The expansive Sinai has been returned to Egypt, but some part of the West Bank and parts of Golan Heights captured from Syria are still retained by Israel. Now the major Arab nations Egypt, Kuwait, Saudi Arabia and Jordan have recognised Israel, but the Palestines will not accept that reality. The other contentious issues like the West Bank, Gaza and Golan settlements remain, but negotiable. The Palestines press for the return of these strips also from Israel but the former still make no commitment that they are willing to accept and recognise the reality of Israel and that they will live in peace with that country. Palestine never make this commitment. The general feeling in the diplomatic world is that 'peace' is not a condition favoured and wanted by the Arab fundamentalists. They fear that with the coming of peace,

Muslims in the Middle East will lose their political philosophy and lose their identity also.But peace is a pre-requisite for economic progress and national reconstruction and even for people eager to go to war, a peacetime is essential even for making war and building the military machine.But the Middle Easterners do not want peace at all. They want war, violence and turmoil and they cannot compromise with permanent peace. Always the Palestine's ask for more new terms. Yasser Arafat was once considered an Arab moderate and the messiah of peace. But he is proving now evasive and unreliable and every time he changes his conditions, the evident motive being the ultimate skuttling of any of settlement with Israel. Israel, hard-pressed for space, water, and the increasing security burden, wants peace with Palestinians and Arabs, but the more they want it, the more intractable it becomes. Now having re-migrated back to Israel and with more than six million of the diaspora, resettled in the original home land, and having no alternative home land in prospect, they are not expected to surrender their home back to the Arabs. Then can the Arabs hope to push them back into the sea? It is feared that Israel is having nuclear bombs and in a desperate push for survival, they will not even hesitate to use it against Arabs. Then what is the prospect of Arab terrorism succeeding in dispersing the Jews once again. Arabs can succeed only in a miracle, and miracles being heaven sent are, not probable. In spite of all kinds of territorial concessions promised by Israel, the Arabs are asking for an absolute withdrawal to pre-1967 borders. These withdrawals are for small areas only, but the subject of critical bargain. When a negotiated settlement is the only possibility, the parties have to meet halfway as there is no strong point in a negotiation as an ungivable part. Palestines do not want peace and their motive is terror without peace.

11
Colonisation And Its Contradictions – The Bush Policy

Before becoming President, Bush met with a series of failures. As a student, he just scraped through Yale and Harvard. He went to Yale only after he was rejected by Texas University. By this time his father built himself up into an oil magnate of Texas, and thus he was born to wealth and privilege but until he becomes Governor of Texas his life was a study in failures. George W. Bush tried at everything his father tried and succeeded, but he succeeded at none and these failures continued into his forties. Always Bush avoids referring to his drinking days when he came close to wasting his life. He made no varsity team, earned no distinction in the Air National Guard, and was defeated in a run for Congress in 1978. He lost heavily in oil business and he was rescued by his fathers friends in 1983. After that he slipped into drinking. In the American political process, leadership remains a great political mystery. David Frum says that through a strange co-incidence alone he turned out to be the Right man in American politics.

Gerald Kaufman, a leader of the British Labour Party grumbled "Bush-the most intellectually backward American President of my political life-time is surrounded by advisers whose bellicosity is exceeded only by their political, military and diplomatic illiteracy". Saudi Crown

Prince Abdullah says, Bush is the type of person who sleeps at 9.30 P.M. after watching the domestic news. In the morning he reads only a few lines about what is written on the Middle East and the world, due to his huge responsibility. To the left Bush gives the impression of a giddy reckless boob, ready to plunge the world into war, out of ignorance and pique. Democratic congressman Jim Moran condemned the 'Axis of Evil' speech of Bush as reckless. But if Bush is a successful President as conqueror and democratiser, these are the qualities that make a statesman.

A veteran in the White House comments "The Democrats are a party with a lot of little ideas, the Republicans the party with a few big ideas". For Reagan, government is the problem, for Nixon-law and order-Eisenhower-peace and prosperity, but difficult to say where George W. Bush stands. Compassionate conservatism turned out to be not a great idea. Bush the uncertain Peace Time President is a super-war-time leader. American people can freely elect and unelect leaders. America shed her blood for Kuwait and Saudi Arabia in 1991, but after September/11, Saudi Arabia shut down the American air base on its territory and refused to co-operate in tracking down terrorists. Who was there in America when America needed help and there were countries where people can speak freely, elect and unelect leaders and where the law applies equally to all.

Democracy in the Muslim world is a stranger. Algerians tried it in 1962 and but for the army take over, the Islamic fundamentalists would have taken over; If the election is not rigged, who would win in Egypt and Pakistan? Bush was initially convinced that Musharaff can be the next Ataturk, but now he retraces. In October 2001, Muslim extremists exploded bombs, first in the Kashmir Assembly, and killed 38 people. On 13th December, these extremists again attacked India's Parliament. Then two Pakistani nuclear scientists were arrested for passing on information to Osama Bin Laden on WMD. The shoe bomber Richard Reid received the go order to blow up a trans-Atlantic jet liner on December 22 and this order came from Islamabad. A month later, Pakistani extremists kidnapped the Wall Street Journal reporter–Danny Pearl and videotaped his grisly murder. Pakistan was aiding North Korea's clandestine nuclear programme while she is a useful ally of the United States; and what would Bush do with this kind of allies? War is on terror but what do America do with the allying terrorist? The problem is complex, but now terrorists are on the run, and state sponsored terrorism also is on the decline, and they have no safe haven which is permanent retreat.

Saddam Hussein is a nasty piece of fruit from the stinking bowl from Algeria to Kabul. Saddam's most extreme offensive was the attempted assassination of George Bush Sr. when he visited Kuwait in 1993. The battle against the world's most nightmarish dictator could be a matter of Bush family affair, and so it can be faulted. But is there no other guilt for the whole world to charge on the murder machine called Saddam Hussein, who is worse than Joseph Stalin-whose machine looked more articulate? In the great terrorism rhetoric and its counter blasts, are lost the crimes of Saddam Hussein against humanity.

The crime story of American soldiers abusing Iraqi prisoners of war was big news. Some stripped naked, some are exposed and some are obscenely insulted. Those scenes are clearly repulsive to rule of law and morals and the first principles of democracy. But this is not peace, but war. Can the world expect that the military man can behave like a civilian moralist? Can we consider a military prisoner who comes to attack, kill, rape and over-power as entitled to the rules of civil order? Is there a code of morality for the soldier whose aim is to fight and win by any means? The military man is bound by the rules of secrecy and he is protected by those rules. Can a hardened terrorist be persuaded to disclose the secrets of his military by civil questioning? If civil questioning is to be followed, there is no need for interrogation of prisoners at all, as no secret information is going to be divulged by them in a decent civil atmosphere. Here are some abusive photographs. But can we take a single photograph from the military scene which is not abhorrent, inhuman and repulsive? In a military operation, there will be scenes of shooting and bayonetting and murder and all those scenes are filled with agony, convulsions and spasms of death. The shooting is merciless and the death is shocking and the scenes of the battlefield spotted with the dead are a horror site. We see innocent civilians running for cover, but still shot down by the merciless guns. These photos are telecast only to rob George W. Bush of the coming election. War photos filled with torture, persecution, neglect and agony never attract vote for Bush. When the Soviets invaded Hungary and Czechoslovakja and Eastern Europe, the troops were indulging in all kinds of inhuman cruelties on civilian population. They were raping and murdering, with impunity, but Human Rights Conventions could not rescue the victims. In 1945 when Allied troops entered Germany, it was an occasion for revenge, and the rapes and murders they committed ran into hundreds of thousands. What can the media or the humanist do against these atrocities committed by troops coming from the countries of the Bill of Rights. When a paranoid British general, defying the clear instruction of Winston Churchill, in World War II, secretly handed over thousands of prisoners of war kept by them to the Russian troops for slaughter (The Cossacks incident) the rights activists could not raise a finger. Against the atrocities of dictators like Stalin, Ho chi Minh, Mao Tse Tung, Pol Pot, Idi Amin, Pinochet and, and Fidel Castro– the media had no complaints and they kept an honourable silence. No complaint they had against genocides but their vehement complaints were directed against the petty human rights violations in the free world only. Certainly, the media man cannot criticise a dictator because the dictator will send his hatchet man to intimidate or eliminate him. The terrorist and their government will not allow any dissident voice to come out, and so the most ebullient journalist' reserves his opinions for democracy only. This is as though the media man has no grievance against Black Death, but declaring war on cold and fever, and this journalistic selection of the least guilty in democracy is a great misconduct and disservice, but still they persist on their selective silliness. This way they try their most to weaken the power of democracy to defend liberty and then who is the loser.

When the American press was lambasting George W. Bush for prisoner abuse the British Press felt humbled as sidelined from the mainstream of defamatory story-telling, and therefore to reinforce and restore their power, they started conspiring ceaselessly for a new hunt. They too got prisoner-abuse photos and *Daily Mirror*-the mass-circulation tabloid, published these photos accusing the British occupation forces in Iraq as committing abuses of the same pattern as perpetrated by the US troops who are in the dock of international indictment. The British government was stung by these photos and they swung into action and for an immediate enquiry. They checked and re-checked and found out that the photos are fake. The unashamedly guilty *Daily Mirror* published a front page apology and sacked its editor, and the political crisis blew over with a whimper. Like the Indian Tehelka, the media not only report scandals, but manufactures it also. When they search for it is in vain, they do not stop, and they start manufacturing it. This media man is a shameless abuser. They do not have interest in a scandal, unless it is connected with the political top brass. They want to pull down only colossuses. They lie in wait as political terrorists, preferably to shoot at the VIP, and their weapon is always simple-the defamation called the scandal; so easy to let loose and so difficult to control.

Is it enough if an apology is printed by *Daily Mirror*? The David Kelly affair brought Blair government to the brink of resignation. The story rose out of the mischief played by the BBC reporter James Gilligan who added the word "sexed up" in the BBC broadcast, and British politics went into tantrums. The Commission of enquiry-Lord Hutton nailed these media cheats– but who will compensate the political injuries of harassment and disrepute caused by the political storm tossing the government? Is it mere fun for a journalist to add words which are politically explosive? These offenders are to be charged for defamation, cheating and treason, but the democratic governments are politically fearful of touching their skin, and so the media man continues to vilify, de-fame and corrupt the truth. They give the message that democracy alone commits sins in the world, and all terrorist and murderous regimes are decent. This is the great disservice done by the media-man who are sheltered wholly in the free world. They live there– fighting the liberty of man.

The impenetrable armour of the media man is that any argument, accusation, condemnation and criticism of the media never find a place in the printed columns or electronic screens controlled by them. The media shut it out at once. Media censuring of news injurious to them is a great challenge to the right to freedom of information. Information should be free, transparent and independent, but this free expression suppressed by the media itself is a contradiction in terms. Presently the media is going intensely all pervasive that all information asked for by the people comes only through them. The journalists are party loyalists also and they screen the news and doctor the writings only to suit their professional interests and loyalties. In this process of winnowing, segregating and classifying of information through human prejudice, the reader is denied his fundamental right to know the truth. Where can he find true information unless it is printed or telecast? But nothing will be exposed, which prejudice, the prejudices of the journalist.

The more cruel nature of the misinformation game is the suppression of news, when vital news is entirely controlled by a caucus who pay no care for the rights of people. Another wrong committed by the media is to publish false information and such falsity has to be contradicted by the victim or another person connected with the incident. But how can he intimate the truth to the reader unless the same newspaper or TV or radio publishes it? Will they do it? They will not do anything that damages their credibility and they try their best to prevent the publication of any contrary information. This is 'media - despotism', and there are millions of misinformation's, false information's and lies traded through print and magnetic channels, but these lies and half truths are received as gospel truth by the majority of the public. This fall in human morals is mainly caused by the media hubris that they, because of mass media control can inform, misinform and disinform the audience, leaving the victim with no remedies in sight.

How was the military photos leaked out in Iraq? It must be with the connivance of the military personnel playing politics inside the barracks. I would say that any photo taken from the camp of prisoners of war will appear offensive to the civil conscience of man. Again I repeat that the highest form of human rights violation is killing a man without cause. In a war situation there may occur a lot of avoidable killings, but no one complains that these shootings are crimes, when they are in fact the cruellest crime. But when there is molestation, teasing, sexual harassment, physical violence, hard labour, whipping etc. the opposition and the media raise a storm of protests. True the Americans and the British did these wrongs in Iraq. But what happened in the prison camps of Russia, Czechoslovakia, China and Japan ? What happened to the American prisoners of war in the Korean War who were detained in China? The treatment was worse as the stories unfold but they allowed none to peep into those cells. The American and British prison camps in Iraq and Afghanistan are considerably better places, but they allow intruders and spies. Surprising how the journalists or congressmen could compare civilian life with the life of a prisoner of war. Did America treat the Japanese and the German prisoners of war in the Second World War in the civil law method? They were all treated with the cruelty and impunity usually practised in war. There were all kinds of harassments and abuses committed by the conquering forces of America, Russia, France and England during their re-conquest of Germany. But in that terrible situation nobody will talk of the decencies of civil law. Now the American Congress and the journalists, because of their awful leisure, are wasting their energies in doing the post mortem on wars in Iraq and Afghanistan. When warriors are all dead, the war on post- mortem is the next thing. These detractor's are not champions defending the rights of Iraqis. If George W. Bush is re-elected in the next November, these wolves will again withdraw into their holes.

12
A Controversial Court Decree Appoints Bush Jr. As President

I started this book on the premise that Gorge W. Bush is a very able leader of America. He was born to privilege, but not a brainy child who will be eagerly picked up by an educational institution of excellence like Stanford of MIT. He qualified in law; but did not go to court to wage his battles in litigation. He tried his ill-luck in oil business, but foundered and rescued from bankrupcy by his father's friends. Unlike his impending electoral opponent John Kerry, he is not a combatant hero of Vietnam War. He enjoyed those exemptions which a highly privileged father commands, but never a spoilt child in spite of running often to the brink. He smoked marijuana but rescued himself, may be because of change of heart, and it is assumed to be assumed that he was not prosecuted by reason of his high connections. But he is a devout Christian and believer in god, and even in the White House he issues Christian admonitions against half believers. It is his mother who disciplined his religious life and often he rejoins the company of the famous evangelist, Billy Graham.

He ran to his forties with almost nothing achieved as stepping stone for a tumultuous political career of imperial conquest, annexation and political fame. He ran for Congress in the eighties but trounced and humbled, but did not give up. Then comes the breakthrough in 1994-when he ran for Texas governor and won. His wife Laura says he is excellent at his timings, and he plays wonders. But all his timings failed to click till 1994, when he defeated the incumbent governor Ann Richards-who as governor of Texas was a very able administrator. There was the gun control law on the anvil and Ann Richards refused to ratify it because it permits students to carry revolvers to school. But in the Bush victory this law was crucial and he promised to sign it into law and he won. The many proud fathers of gun carrying wards voted for him. So the son of a president of the United States is becoming a state governor, and he can now set his sights high to the Oval office. But will the people of the United States accept him? He has the team and strategy but luck is an important factor. In 1998, he was re-nominated to run for Texas Governor again, and the electioneering was master-minded by Karen Hughes who did the ground work and manipulated the strategy. This time it is more important because rejection of a second term will spoil his chances for the Republican nomination of 2000. This formidable Karl Rove-Karen Hughes team cannot founder, and they led Bush into a second term victory-and he is now placed in the shortlist and to the unstoppable course to wrest the Republican nomination of 2000, for presidency. Many will try to indict that his father's wealth helped him greatly to place himself at the centre stage. True, wealth is wealth and it facilitates on many occasions, but not always. Bush proved a tough administrator as Governor of Texas. There is the story of a woman convict, sentenced and facing the death-row in Texas prison. She is a born-again Christian, while in prison and a Christian delegation comprising pious members came to plead with Bush to spare her life by granting pardon. Bush examined the case and asked some questions which the delegates could not answer but only grumble at. He rejected the mercy petition and that born again was executed for her complicity in a multiple murder. What kind of administrator is George Bush, this story makes it very clear. He is tough on law and order, and refuses to mix religion with politics.

Bush launched a powerful campaign for Presidency in 2000, when Al Gore–the Democratic opponent, stood suffering the bad reputation of serving the scandalised but outgoing Clinton administration. The Clinton impeachment and the Lewinsky episode were lambasting the Democrats and from this bad name the party was reeling and the burden fell heavily on Al Gore to prove not his innocence, but the innocence of his unimpeached superior. Clinton came to be identified with sin and it gave a difficult time for Al Gore. The retrospect tells that the Sr. Bush presidency was rebuked and rejected by the American people for the surrender mania gripping that administration and such recall of the past will be big liability for Bush Jr. True, Bush Jr. was elected governor of Texas twice and he had established himself capable to govern. A son of Lincoln or FDR campaigning for presidency would have been greatly pushed and accelerated by the halo of their famous fathers but that halo will not work for Bush Jr. Americans believe that Bush Sr. surrendered in Iraq and so they repudiated him in the re-election though re-elections are easy occasions for incumbents. Then what is the advantage inherited by George W. Bush? Except money, it was the disadvantage of a discredited father, an unbrilliant academic record; and no Vietnam credentials. His opponent Al Gore is a gentleman, but still not many national factors enabling his election, Bush campaign team was a repeat performance of the Texas elections and Karen Hughes and Karil Rove took the weapons out of their political armoury one by one and fired the broadsides, and they could almost level with Al Gore. It looked a neck-to-neck race, but Al Gore got 5,80,000 more votes than George W. Bush, but it was popular votes only, and not electoral votes. Electoral vote is constitutional devise for unmaking a majority vote. In the popular vote count Florida state was found to hold the key, and things came to a head that he who wins Florida will win the presidency. In the first count Bush got a small lead and majority. The first count was challenged by Al Gore, and a recount was ordered. In the recount Al Gore got a lesser lead and smaller majority. But the Bush team challenged it again and in the next recount Bush is again getting a majority vote. Every recount produced a new American President, and the matter went to the Florida courts and there also came conflicting decrees, and the American President election was running into a mess and the country's reputation as a great democracy also came under cloud. The super-democracy of the superpower was failing to pickup her chief executive, and a constitutional crisis is in the offing. As the election of Jefferson in 1800, it was feared that the choice may land in the House of Representatives who will have to elect the new President from the top contestants.

The legal battle in the state courts continued and went inconclusive. The matter was taken to the highest court. The Supreme Court disapproved of the game plan of Florida courts, and the election authorities. The high tribunal declared that once a count is made, a recount can be ordered by the election authority only on clear proof that the first count was wrong. Here the second count was made merely for the asking, and when, the election hangs on a hair thin margin, it will be inexpedient and speculative to engage in the game of continuous re-counts, as every re-count may produce a new winner and the candidates forced into the dangerous alternatives of agony and ecstasy. This is not the aim of a fair ballot and ordered that the first count is valid and the court set the controversy at rest. The court in effect declared George W. Bush as winner and the presidency this time is a gift of the court. As his friends, opponents and biographers say, he was lucky. But luck alone does not make a President. Now he must be lucky as well as competent.

George W. Bush today is America's war captain who conquered and subjugated the ancient lands of Afghanistan and Iraq. His father George H.W. Bush also succeeded in invading and capturing Iraq in 1991, but he failed in the main task the punishment and overthrow of Saddam Hussein–the cruellest dictator alive. When Bush Sr. surrendered Iraq back to the dictator on a platter, the American people were distressed to see their President changing a great victory into defeat, and an alarmed nation , voted him out. So the present Bush inherits the notorious legacy of surrender instead of victory, and he is trying once again to convert that defeat into victory.

Regarding the 2003 Iraqi war, the main provocation has been the September/11, attack on the Twin Towers in New York, by Al Queda killing more than 3000 innocents who are Americans and non-Americans. Bush lost no time to speak and vow for revenge by speedy and massive retaliation. He first attacked Afghanistan and threw out the Taliban, and the governance of the country was entrusted to a local council. Reforms have been initiated throughout the country, but the task of converting a religious fundamentalist society into a modern society requires courageous, careful as well as complex efforts at diplomacy, planning and execution. There the theocratic opposition and its hurdles are considerable though not so intense as Americans are now experiencing in Iraq. The slogan 'Afghanistan for Afghans' worked well in that country and the terror of a guerrilla war that drove the Soviet to despair is not facing the United States. But the same strategy when applied in Iraq is suffering much strain and unexpected challenges. The President is now busy fighting the guerrilla war unleashed by Iraqi terrorists, and this war hampers the re-construction of Iraqi economy. Many Congress sanctioned billions remain unexpended on 27th June 2004, when the Interim Governing Council took over from the Anglo American Coalition.

When Bush Sr. went to Kuwait to liberate that land from the Iraqi-stranglehold the international community, stood solidly behind the United States. The then attacking force comprised the forces of United States, Britain, Germany, France, Australia, Italy etc. Saudi Arabia allowed America to open several military bases in her territory, but certain terrorist outfits and America-haters like Syria, Palestine, Libya etc only opposed. Japan did not send troops, but agreed to share the war expenses. But in spite of this consolidated and unified approach by the partners, the First Gulf War failed only because of the indecision of Sr. Bush. By then the resolute Margaret Thatcher had disappeared from power in Britain and John Major, who just entered was a mismatch for the job. The unique Reagan-Thatcher combination during the Falklands war is no more there. Of course the decisive role shall be that of the United States but her President is vacillating. Then contrast the First Gulf War with the Second. In the Second Gulf War, Germany and France left the coalition saying that the war is ill-timed and unnecessary. The German Chancellor Schroeder has made the revolt only to win re-election but it is still a revolt. French President-Chirac is haunted by Gaullism.

Saudi Arabia changed much since 1991 and she is no more pro-America. Kuwait is not under Iraqi occupation and the Arab world is not as much worried of Saddam as in 1991. And they are not worried of state terror and genocide perpetrated by Saddam Hussein, because terror and terror bombings are the primary lessons taught to an Arab politician and political worker. If Saddam has killed 5000 Kurds by poison gassing, the Arabs find nothing extra-ordinary in it, and human rights violations are not a political crime for them to protest. When genocide and terror are socially accepted methods of political activity, there is no compulsion to move the people of Middle East against Saddam. Then how can America find excuses to dethrone Saddam and establish a political order through free and fair elections? In the whole Middle East, there is no Arab country which is ruled by a government elected through a free and fair ballot, or any kind of ballot at all. The very crucial question is why the Anglo-American governments want to establish a democratic regime, when the people themselves are indifferent to the laws of democracy. Only in the nearby Muslim country–Turkey, there is an elected government, but the Arab League is not in talking terms with that country, which the great Muslim reformer Ataturk himself has founded. Can George W. Bush–the white man become the Ataturk of Iraq? He can only imitate, and how much he can imitate and succeed is a case in American determination. Is George W. Bush resolute enough, and that is the question.

13
The Iraqi Marshall Plan And The Terrorist Revolt Against

Already there are signs of slow down in the re-construction and democratisation plans of George W. Bush. Much work is done in Iraq on restoration of law and order and normalisation. The hospitals have started working and the educational institutions have opened and students are free. The women are moving into markets. Free food supply has made much headway, communication and power supply are restored. If the re-construction work is continued unopposed and un-hampered, Iraq in the near future can be a very wealthy country once again by tapping its huge oil wealth, and cultivating the fertile delta of the legendary Euphrates and Tigris. But the people of Iraq are told to believe that in order to frustrate the Anglo-Americans, the Iraqis shall fight them. An American authorised economy and society, however prosperous and advanced, is not in the interests of Iraqis, and so those plans are to be fought and defeated, the rebels contend. The Germans, after World War II did not fight the Marshall Plan but co-operated with it and they prospered in high speed. The Japanese joined with Mc. Arthur and prospered into the second biggest economy of the world within twenty years. The developing world stand in queue to get American money and technology to grow into super-economies. Then why not Iraq also accept the same? Americans are willing to handover fully, once law and order is restored and a really governing-self-government is established in Baghdad. But the terrorists want to wreck all these plans. They fear the restoration of law and order; they fear economic development, they fear freedom and democracy and they want to prevent any occasion that permit the Iraqi's to taste the benefits of freedom and the fruits of economic development. They fear also that once democracy is established in Iraq, the fundamentalists will have no place there, and that is the motive, guiding the terrorists. There is no democracy in the whole of the Middle East and any kind of democratic liberalisation will be a threat to all regimes around. Democratisation is feared not only by anti-western Middle Easterns but by pro-western Middle Easterns like Saudi Arabia, Kuwait, Egypt and UAE also. So to prevent the birth of a democratic republic, almost all regimes in the Middle-East are united in a powerful conspiracy.

Can we say that terror-bombings represent the will of the people of Iraq? The popular will shall be otherwise. All people want to be free and want the right of a self-determination and the only effective way of expressing that determination is the free-ballot. The Anglo-American authorities proclaim they are ready to quit Iraq once a legitimate self-government is installed in Baghdad. This promise they made in Europe and Japan and in other places and they scrupulously kept their word and their occupied territories are now some of the most powerful democracies in the world. Why can't the Iraqis believe these words? No doubt they believe these words as true and that is the problem. They fear Iraqi freedom and so fight the decision. What they fear is democracy, prosperity and liberty and so they fight the programme as unIslamic and anti-prophet. Also they fear that once freedom arrives with the people they will throw away religion and terror. Vested interests fear that under freedom their interests are fundamentally imperilled.

The culture of democracy is against the culture of the Middle East. Bringing democracy to Iraq may be a ruinous development so far as the Iraqi fundamentalists are concerned. The Iraqi terrorist places religious fundamentalism in front, and put freedom in the back-burner and the occasion they fear the most is the occasion when Iraqis make their free expression. The terrorist wants to establish their rule through fear of terror and they think the more bombs are exploded to intimidate the citizen, the more their chance to win. This puts the Anglo-American authorities under great strain. America wants to withdraw from Iraq at the earliest opportunity but can they leave behind a state in utter disorder and anarchy? But as in Vietnam, they will have to do the same in Iraq also, if the Iraqi revolt is gaining more momentum. Once they leave Saddam behind there is no guarantee that he will not come back to power and take terrible revenge on those whom he will take as scape goats. Then, will not Bush Jr. be condemned by the same accusation which defeated his father in the re-election of 1992? Will George W. Bush also execute the second surrender before Saddam ?

If America, after handing over power on 27th June 2004, had left Iraq lock, stock and barrel, the Iraqi common man's hopes for freedom, development, prosperity and good government will go in smoke. A June 27 total withdrawal would have been the greatest breach of promise by America after Jimmy Carter refused to salvage the Shaw of Iran and surrendered that country to the terror machine of Ayatollah Khomeini. Carter had to witness the wholesale slaughter of citizens and military men by Ayatollah and the American prestige in the Middle East sinking to hell. When Shaw went, America lost her staunchest ally there and America emerged as the unreliable master ally. When terrorists took 53 American hostages in Tehran and the drama continued for months challenging American power, Carter was executing an isolationist retreat from global responsibilities. He was instability and fear-complex incarnate. In the Carter years, the entire free-world stood threatened by the military activism of Russia and China and even western Europe looked threatened by a Soviet take over. What do the Iranian crisis tell the world? The success or failure of the free world ultimately depends on the person of the American President. George W. Bush is a courageous, motivated ruler, who wants to keep America not only a superpower because of her arsenal, but superpower because of her battling courage. You will ask why an Indian comes forward so partisan to praise George W. Bush–a ruler on the other side of the globe. The answer is simple. Imagine America disappears tomorrow? What will happen to world democracies of which India is the biggest? Suddenly democracies will become unsafe. Every free man has a duty to speak for the defence of the free world. The debacle in Vietnam looms large to threaten the American endeavour to create a free Iraq.

Did George W. Bush do a right thing for American democracy by invading Iraq and overthrowing the tyrannical regime of Saddam Hussein? This, according to the laws of war and the law of battles look more mysterious than real. Considering the law of nations as interpreted by jurists, one state has no right for armed intervention in another state and so the law will say it is illegal to attack Iraq. However, if America was defending its security and as a matter of active defence or preventive offence, the above plea can have a questioned validity in the eyes of international law. In 1991 also, the same question arose. Iraq then committed aggression on Kuwait and in a swift blitzkrieg, Kuwait was captured, occupied and taken over by Iraq. The duty then cast on international community was to liberate Kuwait. Many nations including Europe, Australia, Canada and Japan, joined the war of liberation. And like occupation, liberation also was quick on fast track. Kuwait was liberated but Saddam Hussein was left in power and left free to torture and murder Iraqi people once again. The Iraqi dictator continued in power, and this retention was interpreted as the most mysterious surrender executed by George Bush Sr. Iraq was notionally placed under the supervision and control of the United Nations but Saddam could operate his terror-machine and dominate his opponents both real and imaginary. He prevented UN supervision and acted with vengeance.

But the war of 2003 has been won by George Bush Jr. and Saddam has been deposed but remember Saddam is in Iraq. Saddam is overthrown and captured and he is in American captivity and in physical detention in some American military base there. America already handed over power to an Iraqi Interim Council, but what will happen to the Saddam trial is in under suspense. The new government in Iraq may put the ex-dictator on trial, and perhaps he may be awarded the death penalty also, which is now statutorily revived. But the question facing the Coalition is a high dilemma once again. After his capture, the Saddam trial ought to have been the top priority of the Coalition, but America is said to be interrogating him again and again to gain more information. After his capture, what is the usefulness of information elicited from him through a long interrogation? Is it to write his long biography? These details are available through, many other sources like lay witnesses to his terror-reign. But again the most vital question go unaddressed. Saddam, once handed over to the new regime in Iraq, the game of politics begins. Unless the United States controls the security apparatus and exercise effective custody on the body of Saddam, there is no guarantee that the much-vaunted Saddam trial will go to the ultimate, logical finish. If America relaxes its controls, the new and native Iraqi regime will be forced and disposed to a compromise on the body of Saddam. And not impossible such compromise may involve a clause for his release also; or he may slip away from government control and go under ground again to re-organise his forces. If released from custody there is the very dangerous possibility of the Arab world rallying around him, as the spectacular hero of torture and genocide–the acts glorified by the hero-worshippers in the Middle East. Bush shall know that his latest soft pedaling on Iraq, mainly advocated, endorsed and abetted by the inimical media, the born enemy of any powerful presidency, may affect his chances for re-election. John Kerry–his Democratic opponent is talking ill of every-thing Bush stands for because Kerry has to oppose Bushism to survive in the poll-battle. For the re-election win for Bush, an early Saddam trial and punishment would have been helpful. If kept as a celebrated prisoner, even this mass murderer can acquire a halo for political respectability and restoration. But under the election shadow, the President stands jolted and unnerved, and his plans for Iraq are going soft. Having to change his plan according to opinion polls is an unbearable ordeal. The first thing Bush ought to have prioritised is the trial of Saddam. If

Bush wants to win he should feed to the popular sentiment, Victory is possible when the enemy is finally defeated and what is a final defeat? If the President does not know what it is, then the American people know it. Because of the imminent poll, Bush Jr. is submitting to media pressure which may be a serious mistake. Ignore the media and take the war to a triumphant conclusion and America will recognise his courage. Has any ruler won a war by deferring to the wishes of mediaman, who has no advice to offer except criticism? The mediaman is no Napoleon and his concern is as firm as institutional, and that is the failure of America everywhere. When you win the war, the shameless mediaman will swallow all the words vomited earlier, and unashamedly, will mount the wagon of victory parade.They criticised the Vietnam War to the extent of treason, and Nixon wavered and then surrendered to them. If Nixon had ignored Watergate and prosecuted the mediamen, and ignored the congressmen who opposed the war, there would have been no Watergate, and no dishonourable surrender in Vietnam. But Nixon did not possess that courage or political wisdom, and he wavered and then collapsed. The main enemy of American victory any-where is the media, and secondly a jealous Congress controlled by the opposite party of the President. This is the time for Bush to act. If he acts tough, there will arise a hornets' nest of criticism and condemnation, but all this disappears if he is re-elected. The investigative journalist is the weapon of the left to persecute the right, and those who have paid heed to their criticism have been finally deceived. This is the misstep executed by Nixon in Watergate. When the media mercenaries like Woodward and Bernstein and congressional sharks like Peter Rodino and Sam Ervin came demanding the blood of Nixon, the latter threw away his loyal lieutenants one by one to the wolves hoping to pacify them. But these wolves, tasting blood once, came back with animal ferocity and demanded more and more blood, and at last Nixon was left with no genuine supporter. On the other hand, if Nixon had ignored these demands and stood by his confidants, and refused steadfast to appoint any a special prosecutor, Watergate would have died down. Bush should learn this lesson and direct blows on political opponents without grace. You must retaliate against the enemy, who conspires your downfall. Still there is time and if you act with determination, you can do it once more in November 2004.

14
Whether September/11 Could Have Been Prevented? That Awful Speculation

Of late, as usual, a frustrated team of betrayers are entering the political highway to attack the President. Richard Clark–the counter terrorism guru of Clinton and George W. Bush himself contends in his new book that the Bush Presidency is mere humbug, and the attack on Iraq was predetermined. He fails to mention that the Iraqi dictator was once allowed to escape by Sr. Bush only on wrong advice, and this top terrorist was granted a new lease of life by America. But the free citizens of America will not reconcile with the Bush surrender in 1991 and so the President was unseated in the poll. Now the son-Bush is in office. The same Saddam though in captivity, is commanding a guerrilla war in Iraq when America goes to polls in November 2004.

Clark argues that Sr. Bush and Clinton have neglected the terrorist threats though information was available regarding the growing power of Al Qaeda, which crime syndicate was incorporated as early as 1990. Sr. Bush completely ignored it. Clinton had made plans to counter terrorist threats, but he was hamstrung by sex scandals, and failed to make headway. When George W. Bush came to office in 2001, Clark says, he made repeated demands to insiders like Donald Rumsfeld, Condoleezza Rice, Dick Cheney etc to prioritise a preventive strategy and action plan but they failed to react, as those people were plunged heart and soul in the Iraqi question, even though Iraq was not then the spring board of terrorism. Truly it was Afghanistan. Clark says if his advice had been heeded, September/ 11, would have been avoided. But he fails to explain why he continued in the indicted administration so long when he could not shape any concrete counter-terrorism scheme in the Bush White House. He does not directly accuse Bush for failure to prevent the September/11 attack, but there is a joint accusation that many Presidents–Reagan, Bush Sr., Clinton and Bush Jr. are all responsible, being careless to attend to the urgency. He further accuses that all his pleas fell on deaf years initially and every demand was ignored.May be those responsible were unimpressed of his pleas for preventive action and they could never imagine the high-tech, the improbable and the horrible tragedy caused through planes hijacking on September/11, 2001.

What is the terrorist's operational style? There is no open war waged, which is easy to meet, when it is a shooting war. But there is the vehement plea that the September/11 attack was the result of official complacency. As discussed earlier, the attack is a secret operation and any skyscraper in New York or Chicago or Houston or anywhere in the United States could be targeted. This is not merely bombing, but a special, novel raid, hitherto unknown and untested. The world saw so many hijackings and its human tragedies; there were ultimatums to shoot the captives, unless the demands are met. There are storm troopers rushing in under the cover of negotiations or darkness, and rescuing captives; and there are states surrendering to the demands, and there are hijackers paid huge ransoms to withdraw the other demands. The negotiations are high-drama as well as highest adventure. The Israeli release of Jewish hostages from Emtebbe airport in Uganda remains the most spectacular rescue adventure in the history of hijackings.The year long Iranian hostage drama in 1979 and the Russian hostage drama in the Moscow Theatre remain unique challenges.The common method of terrorists is bombing and killing innocents. Bombing passengers and car bombings are the more popular methods in Iraq. But terrorists have become more safety conscious and avoid open encounters, and of late suicidal bombings and car bombings take a heavy toll. Recently hijackings have come down as airport security has been strengthened through out the world. But the airline operators in America seriously objected to flight restrictions being placed on the travelling public and so there were plenty of loopholes left out for hijackers to penetrate the flight regimes. The US airline operators contended that too many restrictions on air travel will drive away passengers to other modes of less-speedy travel like car and train and so they resisted.The terrorists took advantage of these loopholes, and the result was September/11.

New innovations are added and tested by the terrorists to breach security blankets and they sharpen and revise their techniques continuously. It is true that the CIA and the FBI had distilled much information regarding Al Qaeda, but was there any definite information that planes are going to be hijacked and these planes are to be used as missiles to crash on populous skyscrapers like the World Trade Centre in New York or the Sears Tower in Chicago or what not. There could have been more security tightening in airports and air transport, but that was not done on considerations of commercial viability and passenger inconvenience. This failure now stares at the authorities. But once a plane is hijacked, it is going to be used as missile against any skyscraper is a novel idea for which, without clear prior-information, definite counter measures could not be taken. The information that reached CIA and FBI did not give a clear warning about the modus operandi, but after the attack any one can accuse any one else for failure to act. For any national calamity, the government will be found fault with always. Crime prevention is only a defensive action and preventing modern day terrorism is like preventing modern day theft. When a dacoity is committed, we are alerted to the shortcomings even in the best of security arrangements. When a house is burgled, the neighbour will ask the owner why he left the house unguarded while going away! But human nature as it is, man is often negligent and lax towards preventive measures. We can only strengthen the security of the future and not the security of the past. But what do the September/11 Commission say? They want to unmake the past and reinvent it. They contend that security measures ought to have been more imaginative and stronger. What is the historic expediency of this argument? True, Bush and his advisors have failed to catch the warning signals which the CIA and the FBI deliberately wanted to suppress, or distort or misinterpret. But there is no denial of the fact that no clear idea regarding the modus operandi of September/11 could be gathered before hand. Then what kind of precaution is to be taken? America can mobilise her whole armed forces at home and abroad to meet the challenge, but what is the actual target none can say. The United States armed forces at home and abroad cannot be put on mobilisation for catching a lone hijacker. If CIA got information that the WTC is going to be immediately blasted, then even one American war plane was sufficient to stop the terrorists. When Hitler showed his power in Munich it was vain for Chamberlain to appease him, because the war horse was already on rampage. The September/11 Commission is enquiring whether the tragedy could have been averted. If the Twin Towers had been well guarded, Al Queda would never come to New York, but would go elsewhere. Here the terrorist wants to hit the most reputed target as they want to get the highest publicity, and if that target is unavailable, they will choose a less reputed one.

Different statesmen avail different policies and strategies to meet the enemy, and some will be profoundly effective and punishing, whereas some ineffective as well as frustrating. We cannot re-create the past. Then why the American Congress does it? It becomes customary for Congress to conduct national inquests into calamities and tragedies, and that is their very important forte. It all started with the St. Chair expedition into Indian territory, and thereafter institutionalised through congressional preferences only. Mainly these are on corruption charges and misdemeanors, but one illegal aspect is that such enquiries never end, and often outstrip the presidential term which is the subject matter of enquiry. America had Tea Pot Dome, Mc Carthy Watergate, Korea-Gate, Iran Contra, White Water etc which were not stopped by the plea that such public interrogation and media trial strip citizens of their fundamental rights and basic rights. These rights–gifts of nature rather than gifts of God–cannot be interfered with.Congress may not act as the Grand Inquest of the nation, in all cases but that is a different question not very relevant here. Now too many people and think-tanks argue that the government of the United States had not taken any extraordinary steps to prevent this very extraordinary tragedy. But none told the President or Secretary of State that Al Qaeda would hit and destroy the Twin Towers at Ground Zero. In a great war, it is possible for a country to give an ultimatum to the invader that the former will side with the victim. But many nations, fearing the uncontrollable escalation of war, refuse to give an ultimatum because that itself will prejudice the stand of the opponent. Al Qaeda decided to attack a vital point in the United States and if it failed today, they will aim a different target. The world has seen many victories and defeats, but nowhere has the aimless search for redoing the past been so vociferously and emphatically pursued except in the United States.Is there any worse wastage of human work and talent than searching for the errors of the past which we have committed unintentionally? But America does it, and her energy and resources are wasted aimlessly, simply for unmaking the past and this is an American speciality.

Democracy is accused of many basic weaknesses, and the critics include philosophers like Plato and Aristotle, down to modern political theorists. They say democracy is weak in confronting and managing emergencies, and they criticise its in-capacity to act with promptitude and decisiveness. The system is always weakened by insubordination, internal dissention and disregard of authority. It frequently resorts to violence, bringing in anarchy and readying to welcome military tyranny. It suffers from fickleness and instability, frequent changes of opinion and the consequent confusion in the conduct of state affairs. It abets a desire to level down, and quite regrettably intolerant of greatness. Popular opinion leads to majority opinion and this leads to the tyranny of the majority over the minority. (Now the new version of this dogma is the tyranny of the minority over majority). It incites the passion for changing customs and destroying old institutions, and there is an irrational and irrepressible love for novelty. Political ignorance leads to political deception, and consequently the masses are misled. This condition sets up demagogues to play on the passion and selfishness of the masses; and the comments of great critics go on like this.

As leader of the free world, the American democracy has a special duty to reply these political as well as philosophical misgivings of great men. American democracy is the de facto guardian of freedom, and the leader of the free world. But the surprising aspect is that while America suffers all these faults and innuendos, it survives. How does it survive after committing all these faults which are fatal to many western democracies like France, Italy and Germany? Political philosophers say that this is due to America having no aristocracy: The other reason is the blessings of abundant resources, and I will reiterate that point. There is no vigil and anxiety in America on their existence comparable to the restless vigil maintained by a country like Israel on her survival. Israel is surrounded by enemies, but America is surrounded by dependents, well-wishers, collaborators and petty revolutionaries. She could wage any number of wars, and lose it all but still remain undefeated. She will lose any number of battles, but still her home land is as undisturbed as peace. She is the only superpower, but she maintains the knack for innumerable surrenders; and she terrifies the world not by her victories but by her defeats. The more she surrenders the more she becomes dominant in world affairs. Harry S. Truman, had not the determination and blood-thirst of Joseph Stalin–to demand the surrender of the whole world in

1945–when America alone possessed the nuclear bomb. Lucky we are that America got the first bomb and American democracy has no political programme for liberating the Iron Curtain countries. America fails in all her adventures but what is the secret of her hegemonic stature still ? It is a mystique and that mystique continues to surprise.

After the Civil War, many European philosophers feared that some northern general will emerge and take over America. But immediately after the end of hostilities the great generals like Grant, Lee and Sheridan were forced into huge public receptions, and they were made into popular heroes. Close on heels came the disbandment of the armed forces and the huge army disappeared over-night, and the civil authority superseded them. But all things do not happen by design. It happened by luck also. Geographically and economically, America is exceptionally lucky. Hamilton, who was the mastermind of the American nation, persuaded the state delegates at Philadelphia to exceed their instructions and vote for a Constitution empowering the founding of strong federal (Union) government. He visioned that only a strong centre can advance the future interests of American democracy. The bad and anarchical experiences of the Articles of Confederation had created an awareness for a more solid union, but the states were suspicious of a central authority or President, who may turn into a monarch or dictator, and this argument continued with force. Americans fought united against the British, and a united fight meant the idea to establish a union of states for founding a strong central government. The absence of Jefferson in the Philadelphia Convention of 1787 also facilitated the plea of Hamilton to succeed. Jefferson, then minister in Paris was for a weak union and strong states. The French Revolution was raging before his eyes in Paris, and he was enjoying it. Hamilton had the backing of Washington–the President of the Convention. Once the delegates voted for a strong union, the next question was who shall be the real ruler of America. Should America have a President or a committee of Presidents. The multi-member French Directory (which came only much later) was not there then to strengthen the arguments for a single-man presidency. The prospect of Washington becoming the first President also helped the consensus for a single man presidency. American history says that, in the entire constitutional structure there is no better arrangement to strengthen the union than opting for an one-man chief magistracy. The multi-member Directory assuming the reigns of power in Paris after the French Revolution ended in disaster. At last the delegates voted for a single President and Washington was the inevitable choice. No doubt his stature and popularity also contributed to the growth and power of the Presidency as the singular and outstanding representative of the country in future years. That office, in a short while, grew into the real representative of the Union, and America came to be known through her Presidents. The rise of the presidency was due mainly to the growth of the federal government, and the person who later helped the most the growth of the union is John Marshall, the great Chief Justice. He had the long tenure of thirty-four years, and in him resided the duty to reinvent an orderly and powerful republic. Not only that he invented and established the power of judicial review, he invented a powerful federal government also. But for his commerce clause interpretation, the most powerful United States would never have been born, much less a powerful Supreme Court who diligently watches the rule of equal protection under law. Judicial decisions are a restraint and brake on the adventurous courses of a ruler, but in judiciary also, United States makes new history. American contributions are varied, and there are so many bests in her politics, law, economics and technology, that supported the formation of the most powerful economic and military power on earth, producing a political and military superiority that leads the world.

Sensing the spectacular rise of economic growth and its potential, in the course of the 20th century there were commentators who predicted that Japan and Soviet Union will overtake United States both economically and militarily. Soviet Union collapsed due to its unnatural political formula and Japanese growth slowed into recession. Brazil, because of her land mass and rich resources, was often cited as a political competitor to America but in spite of her long period of freedom, she remains in the background. When we reach the twenty-first century, there is a better competitor to U.S., Communist China. China maintains a high growth rate by adopting capitalist techniques in a communist society. If things go on in the present way China can overtake the United States by 2040 or 2050 AD. But the biggest risk-factor in China is the political system blocking the freedom of her people. Twentieth century has tasted communism widely and long, and when the Marxian doctrine was put to practical test, it all failed abominably and the world repudiated it, China learnt lessons from Russia and Eastern Europe, and hastily is reforming her economy. Chinese society is thrown open to the world, and the Iron Curtain now tolerates wide breaches in it body. But there is no democracy in China and as far as the political system is concerned, they maintain and operate a one-party state as established by the founder Mao Tse Tung. Can the Chinese protect this political lock-up for ever is a frightening question. Is it possible to maintain an open-jail of this magnitude? If China had been a democracy maintaining the economic discipline of the power-house, a direct challenge to United States and a continuing challenge to her superpower status is a possibility.But in the military field, it may not be possible for China for long to challenge American technology. America, even when overtaken by China in economic quantity, will be capable of maintaining her lead in technology for longer times. This is the political analysis of pundits. It is history that similar predictions on Soviet Union, Japan, Brazil etc. have fallen on the way side and none came up as real competitor to United States. This is the question of economics, but regarding a super-power there are more important questions on this issue. Even Japan could not compete with U.S.A. in spite of the splendid economic progress she made in the sixties and seventies of 20th century. A study of the scientific and technological achievements made by the United States in the 20th century looks very different for any other country to excel it in the 21st century. But the biggest guarantee for American supremacy is her technological eminence. Still her political system and its explosive situation remains a big risk factor for China to contend with in future. When it comes to the people to choose between freedom and wealth, they rush towards freedom, and that behaviouristic selection on human preferences tells badly on the prospects of a Chinese State as super-power. But China can have corrective measures. She can liberalise the political system without unduly upsetting her political economy; or she can directly go for full democratisation, but that step looks unlikely considering the existing political realities. The history of Soviet Union and Eastern Europe say it is impossible to keep a prosperous economy within the dark confines of Iron Curtain. There is real difference between Soviet Union and China in economic approaches. Soviet Union remained a fully closed society till its collapse in 1989, but China takes a different route. The Chinese economy is a fully open commercial society whereas her politics remains closed and despotic. From the present day developments in Hong Kong, the Chinese authorities may wish that they let the British rule Hong Kong for some more decades because to them today's Hong Kong is the enclave of counter-insurgency within the mainland.

15
The European Betrayal

Better than any other system, it is democracy which needs the best talent in governance, but only rarely she receives it. President Bush is regularly accused by the media that he failed in everything he laid hands on till he became Governor of Texas. Also they condemn that he acts on the words of advisers like Karl Rove, Karen Hughes and Condoleeza Rice and Co, and the President, left to himself, is a stupid fellow. These critics fail to note that the most important faculty of a politician is his capacity to govern and lead.Till he became President, he as a seeker of personal fortunes, fate and circumstances seldom smiled on him. Take Lincoln, he was consistently and repeatedly unlucky to get elected to any representative assembly, but he won the presidency directly. A rebuffed Bush hesitantly tried for the Governors ticket in Texas and got it. Quite luckily, Bush sided with gun-runners and he won. His opponent Ann Richards refused to sign a bill permitting guns in schools, and good that the chance gave Bush the opportunity. As Bush was siding with the gun carriage law, now school children in Texas are free to carry pistols in their school bags and their parents are proud of it. Whether Bush is a capable administrator or not, he is lucky to get elected twice to the post of Governor of Texas his own home state. He kept the advisory team who helped him succeed as governor, and this team prepared the strategy for winning the Republican nomination, and most importantly the strategy for winning the presidential vote. Al Gore–the Democratic opponent of 2000 was an experienced follower and deputy of Clinton, but the last days of Clinton caught in the quagmire of disrepute, possibly robbed Al Gore also of a good share of votes. Still Al Gore got half-million votes more than Bush, but failed to secure the majority of electoral votes, and in a stunning electoral upset, Bush was declared elected in a court decree. In the Bush election, the role played by the Supreme Court has been no doubt crucial. Again luckily for Bush, the matter did not go to the House of Representatives as in the case of Jefferson vs. Aaron Burr in 1800, when both secured equal number of electoral votes. At last an unwilling Hamilton helped Jefferson to win, and this dramatic shift by Hamilton enraged Burr, who challenged Hamilton for a duel, and in the bloody encounter with pistols the greatest genius of the American War of independence perished, and Aaron Burr had to sail to European safety. A grievously wounded majoritarian Al Gore did not challenge Bush for a duel. So George W. Bush comes to power. Will Iraq make him an extraordinary President, or has he already made himself into the real leader of the free world. In the First Gulf War 1991, many countries including the whole of NATO supported United States. But now the Bush opponents say that, due to his wrong policies, America is almost a deserted crusader earning the support of her only traditional ally-Britain. What led to this radical change of situation? Democrat John Kerry contends that it is a serious, failure for Bush to have alienated France and Germany. Now the wave of Gaullism is riding Europe, and France wants to proclaim that she is no more the tail of the United States. The unifying force behind NATO was Soviet Union, who is not there. France is joined by Germany led by Gerhard Schroeder. Schroeder was facing an election when the Gulf War Council met in Washington. The pollsters predicted that German people are against their country going to war in Iraq, and so the powerful NATO ally made an unusual break with NATO politics, and succumbing to electoral pressures, decided to keep off Gulf. This break is crucial in determining the NATO priorities also. Schroeder, because of his anti-American stand won re-election. Chirac was riding the Gaullist wave sweeping France, and Europe stands again divided. When the D-Day is remembered on 5th June, 2004 the veterans who committed everything to liberate Europe from Nazi terror were astounded to see the conqueror-Germany standing clasping the hands of France–the vanquished, and opposing the US-British team. History is replete with such stands-off. The Second World War was started by Hitler and Stalin jointly and abruptly they had to part, company in 1941, and Stalin went over to the Allies. There US, Russia, Britain and France fought united and defeated Germany. But after 1945, Russia was building up an anti-free world alliance under an iron clad ideology, and came close to fight the United States. France and Germany went to join US and Britain, out of sheer necessity because of the formers inability to fight and stop a marauding Soviet Union. NATO stood as the solid bulwark against Russia and the Warsaw Pact. The confrontationist ferocity between NATO and Warsaw Pact and their ideological acrimony exposed the world to an almost, nuclear armageddon several times, and this confrontation looked imminent during Berlin Blockade, Korean War and Cuban Missile crisis. But as the greatest mystery of the 20th century, Russia's totalitarian machinery collapsed with a bang in 1989, and it was immediately followed by the fall of communist regimes in satellite countries like East Germany, Hungary, Czechoslovakia, Rumania, Bulgaria and Yugoslavia. The Russian military threat evaporated within days, and a drastic shift in power equations became real and inevitable, and a basic change in the lord-vassal relationship in NATO followed. In the time of De Gaulle himself, a French challenge to American leadership of NATO was declared, and France went swiftly for an independent nuclear strike force.

Comes De-Day Memorial-5th June 2004, when Allied veterans were flocking the Normandy beach to re-enact and remember the victory march that happened sixty years ago. The biggest air borne and amphibious landing force in history was assembled and launched in the Normandy coast to liberate France and other European countries. America was then the saviour and liberator of Europe, but now there is a diametric change of altitudes on the part of France who opposes an American War on Iraq. Germany-which was West Germany till 1989, also is opposing an American War on Iraq following the French lead. But Poland the World War II victim and the most heroic defender in epic confrontations is now a staunch supporter of United States, and she is a new ally to boost US military presence in Iraq. Schroeder won election on the anti-American platform of non-intervention in Iraq, and thus, he stands injuncted by the German mandate on any Iraqi enterprise. Americans ask: in 1944 we came to Noramandy under the heavy artillery barrage of Germans and we suffered thousands of dead, and we were the heaven sent-liberators of Europe. What then about the total dispensability of America in Europe in 2003? The reasons are obvious. Before 1989, if Europe had revolted against US, the Warsaw Pact would come marching against Germany and France. But now the threat of a Soviet led invasion of Europe has vanished and Western Europe is a care free democracy. When threats are over, why they hang on to American dependency? A Russian threat may revive, but only in the distant future. A Chinese threat has to come to Europe only crossing so many Asian countries and also traversing the vast stretches of Russian plains. Any Chinese threat is immediately real only in Asia, as Europe is far away. If the present strategic balance in conventional and nuclear arms is weighed, the Anglo-French nuclear strike force can match the Chinese power. It is the necessity and the wish for survival that forces countries to seek alliances. France and Germany are not quitting NATO, but they are opposed to the military adventures of the United States in Iraq and Afghanistan. France and Germany no more want to be military movers and shakers, but will remain only commercial entities. The latest French crusade has been described by critics as rank ingratitude and political short-sightedness. But why should politics be thankful? Was China thankful to Russia ? Was Russia thankful to America for the huge lend-lease that provided the ammunitions that drove away Germans? The new Franco-German declarations warn the United States that these countries cannot any more be taken for granted. Of the occupied countries in 1945, it is Germany and Japan who shall be beholden to United States. These two countries were recognised, reorganisd and reconstructed and made into modern power houses under massive American efforts. But of all recipients of American aid in the war, it was Soviet Union walking away from Allied camp that was the most cold-blooded but least commented upon. That exit started the Cold War. The present Franco-German volte-face is nothing unusual, considering the cross-routes and the cross-purposes that the erstwhile Allies travelled during the cold war years. It was Winston Churchill who recognised at the earliest the commencement of cold war between the United States-led Free World, and the Russia-led Communist block.The force that forced and shaped the unity of NATO had been the Soviet threat especially, against Western Europe. When Soviet Union broke up, that Communist threat disappeared over-night like mist, and the NATO allies were confronted with an immediate release from cold war obsessions. This was sudden release from bondage and the new situation throws up new military equations. The options are wide and one option as a consequence is that Germany and France, the once powerful NATO Allies can no more be NATO faithfuls.

Bush is facing re-election in November 2004. In the run up we see a powerful and activist President like Bush being hounded by the media and political opponents. Here is the historic truth that the media will never support and recognise a powerful leader, and in any democratic country this is the case. But a powerful President has to act in defence of democracy not because of the media and the Congress, but in spite of they. When United States is the leader of the Free World (and the unrecognised leader of the unfree world too) the situation places serious constraints on non-democratic forces. Imagine a situation of there being no United States at all in the world, and the Free-world comprising only Britain, France, Germany, India etc. China will immediately march towards South East Asia, and after an easy take over and consolidation will next attempt to devour India, Bangladesh and Pakistan. No doubt this will start a bitter cold war between China, Japan and Russia. Then German and Japanese militarism will be forced to revive, threatening the peace of Europe and South East Asia, and Europe will once again be in new security turmoil. The rearmament of Japan will be an inevitable need in the new balance of power, and much more in the balance of terror, and we will be facing the whole Asia in turbulent in-security. In Latin America even one trigger-happy dictator can destabilise the whole continent. Philippines, Australia and New Zealand alone may continue peaceful for sometime, being protected by the waves of the Pacific. Know that the world is never afraid of or serious about the admonitions, resolutions and sanctions of the United Nations. The world lived fearing the balance of terror tactics played between Soviet Union and United States till 1989. After 1989, humanity and their politics are again reconditioned on the hopes and fears of what the United States is saying. It is perceived that the United States can now do what she wants to do, as there is no match for her nuclear might and high technology. From 1989, it is real that the power who can command humanity to obedience is the United States. But the question is whether she makes any effective commands at all. She seldom commands and on most occasions obeys the words of the enemy because most often America gets only weak Presidents like Carter, Ford, Hoover etc.

I reiterated earlier, that America, faces, a specially favourable situation in wars because of her untiring military muscle. After 1815, America, had never been attacked by a foreign military force. When the Second World War ended, the damage suffered by Russia was unimaginably tragic, but still Russia was among the winners. British imperial power has been brought to it knees due to war fatigue, and the country was struggling to stop her empire going for immediate collapse. Japan was so badly beaten that the country lay there in ruins over which the Japanese people stood like ghosts. Germany, Western Europe and Eastern Europe were mere debris, and France lay beaten by occupation. But what happened to America? In spite of fighting the war and suffering large casualties, life in the United States went on normal. There was no famine, no shortage and no disruption to pleasant life. She lost more war-planes and ships than any other country but her normal life has never been disturbed. Before Russia acquired nuclear weapons, America remained absolutely unthreatened, as the nuclear monopolist of the world. Any amount of economic supplies on global scale will not exhaust her resources. She can produce any quantity of munitions that the world wants. War is for her just a peace time operation whereas it is a condition unimaginable for others. History says that there is no country in the world that does not become tired, exhausted, and paralysed due to the demands of war. For any country it is the maximisation of human efforts, but hitherto all American wars had seen only the fractional use of her capacities. The people of that country never experienced the grave dangers and anxieties of a military defeat and foreign occupation. If America failed in Vietnam, that was only due to wrong strategy, irresolution and mob rule, and it never was the end of her fighting power. When United States left Vietnam in 1975, with her residue of armed power, she was capable of waging several Vietnam wars again. But she lost her resolve and determination to take the war to the North. When she turned back in Korea without punishing the aggressor, it was never the end of her resources to fight. American failures and surrenders in 20th century were never due to military compulsions, but on politically weak decisions which remain a basic feature of American domestic politics. For their comfort's sake alone they invented limited wars, and the results had been unlimited defeats. In a war, the new America had two clear options–one to lose voluntarily or to win with surrenders. All these American voluntary surrenders point to the new philosophy of American democracy on war, defeat and victory. When the Allies defeated Germany in 1945, Germany had no other military option as all her resources were reaching the zero point–human and material. But what was the situation when Communists captured power in China in 1949? American power was at its peak with a nuclear monopoly, but weaklings controlled the foreign policy. America having the nuclear monopoly was at abundant advantage, and even by a threat of nuclear strike they could have humbled Mao's fighters. Even Russia could have been humbled by the United States before 1949-when the former stole atomic secrets from the United States. People go to war because war is historic; Also J. B. Priestley says' might is historic and deserves to conquer' and this remains the simple truth even today. Take the case of any war whether in Ramayana or Mahabharata-the Indian epics: or the Hellenic, Mongolian or the modern wars–war comes to an end only because one side is completely exhausted of its resources in arms and men. But America never came to the end of a fraction of her resources even in world wars, but she makes capitulations without defeats. The Berlin Blockade, Chinese Revolution, Korean War, Indo-China war, Vietnam War, First Gulf War, African Civil Wars, the Cuban Revolution, and everywhere America is seen voluntarily surrendering before the least powerful, and such surrender syndrome has become part of American political strategy. What lessons do we learn from voluntary surrenders? America wants to live in comfort, and she is not prepared to disturb that comfort, even if her political class–the free world-is endangered–the very antithesis of what America's founding fathers stood for.

16
Media Plays Into The Hands Of The Enemy

The Second Gulf War presents a revolt in the western camp. This war sowed the seeds of discord in the Western alliance and especially with France and Germany. The French started clashing with American policies immediately on the recall to power of De Gaulle in 1958; and ever since, that confrontation had been growing. After De Gaulle, the independent French policy lacked aim and articulation, but Gaullism continued in low key. In the First Gulf War French joined the team of western forces, but when Bush Jr. started the second assault, the Neo-Gaullist President Chirac came out more assertive. Only because the German Chancellor Schroeder was facing an immediate election that he had to assume an anti-American stand on Iraq this time only to cater to electoral populism. So, with the exclusion of the Big European Two, it was doubted that America will withdraw from the invasion programme. But Bush Jr. was ready for going it alone, and that stand is criticised as unilateralist. Britain stood stead-fast with America and together they attacked Iraq. But the evident motive of the Anglo-America expedition has been the defeat of Iraq, and before the overwhelming invading forces, Iraq collapsed like a pack of cards, and this was no surprise. The Saddam bluff was again called. The so celebrated

Republican Guards of Saddam are either non-existent or vanished into anonymity along with WMD. America and Britain won the war, and Iraq reconquered and taken over by the Anglo-American forces. Now the occupiers want to conduct a free and fair poll. Power is handed over to Iraqi people, but the American army stays there to supervise. Anarchy shows its ugly head in Iraq in the shape of terrorism. But if America wants to make a final quit from Iraq so soon only for the sake of Bush Jr. to win the November 2004 Election, that may not be a safe choice. Leaving Iraq in anarchy will be a second surrender by United States, and such surrender is to be avoided, even disregarding American election results.

What will America do with Saddam and what will be the fate of Saddam when America leaves Iraq? Once Saddam is got back from US custody, the main political question in Iraq will be his release and freedom. But the enormity of his crimes against humanity will be eclipsed by deliberate shadowing by the press and electronic media who always favour tyrants and dictators under the wrong name of revolution. The media stands for human rights, but only in favour of petty rights like teasing, interrogation and nakeding, but not against high crimes, genocides, mass murders and persecutions. Now the crimes of cruel and unusual punishments are already condoned by the media, and they give him a heroic portrayal. Think of the German war criminals at Nuremburg and the Japanese war criminals at Tokyo in 1945. Many were given death penalty and many celebrated prisoners were held in Allied jails indefinitely, most of them dying in prison, after long incarceration. Condoning the crimes of war criminals sends the wrong message. But at that time the people of America and the Congress stood firmly behind Truman for all prosecutions he undertook to punish war criminals. If the famous criminals like Himmler, Hesse, Keitel, Ribbontrop etc in Germany and Tojo and others in Tokyo were handed over to German and Japanese peoples respectively for trial and punishment, what would have followed, none can imagine. Some times the furious victims who suffered so much under them, would have taken them for a mob-trial resulting in law-less tragedies. Also there would have been the dangerous result of these crime-thrillers becoming new heroes, and once again seizing the reigns of power to the shock and dismay of the free world. But the Allies never worked at cross-purposes on this question. They were determined that no criminal shall escape the law, and only under the authorities of the victors that the trial was conducted, punishments pronounced and sentences executed. But now the magnanimous Americans, by handing over Saddam to Iraqi custody are playing a high-risk game. When World War II ended, what was the stand taken by the American media on war criminals, and compare that stand with theirs now on Iraq. In 1945 there was television, but a rare medium and so it was not a force to reckon with; and the main communication highways were the press and radio. The people would never take a stand against War Tribunals as it would be treason, and so the media never ventured into criticising war tribunals. There was little chance of criticising war proceedings in the United States, as people did not favour scandalising the war efforts. Then who is the main war criminal today in the eye of American media? Is it Saddam–the mass murderer or Bush–the liberator? The media is joining the political opponents of Bush in assailing and condemning the war practices of United States-soldiers. Take the war practices of any country in the world including China, Soviet Union, Vietnam or Latin Americas. Is it true that in the war on terror, there will be no prisoner abuse? There is the Geneva Convention on prisoners of war (POW), and it is always violated, and there is no international agency to supervise and punish the violations. Who is there to monitor that the Geneva Convention rules are observed? It is the moral discipline of the State and nothing else. But one unfortunate aspect which fails the people in war practices is the neglecting of serious war crimes and emphasising on petty crimes. If hundred prisoners are shot and killed on silly reasons, that crime is simply ignored, but when one prisoner is abused by teasing nakeding or disrobing it is top news internationally. What is the logic behind this media segregation? When a Hollywood star dies in tragedy, that is simple news, but when her clothes flies off in the wind, that is big news for media. This tabloidisation is doing harm to the role of the fourth estate, and doing greater harm to the rights of man. Do the media think that tabloidisation will reduce the instances of war crimes? Do they believe that mass shootings are lesser crimes than mass teasings? Ultimately, what results is the need for the moral re-education of the media. When all other disciplines need re-education, why not the media also. Geneva conventions can reduce the instances of prisoner abuse, but cannot stop it all, as no penal law stop all crimes.

One important question to the media is on the special pressures exercised by them on President-Bush to windup fast from the Iraqi imbroglio. Bush at times has gone sceptical of winning a second term because of the anti-war hysteria kicked up by the propaganda, un-leashed by Congress, the world media, the American press and television. But there is an important question. Had the next President election been at least three years away, what would have been the chance for an irregular, premature and incomplete handover of Iraqi sovereignty to an Interim Council? What would have happened to Japan if America handed over sovereignty to them immediately after their surrender in August 1945? There would have been mass famine and mass deaths-but being a disciplined and committed people the Japanese would sacrifice anything for reconstruction, but still the misery, penury, want and suffering they would have endured shall have been colossal. So there was no demand from the Japanese, except from a handful of Communists, for an immediate American pull out from that country. Mc Arthur administered Japan for six years, but this long rule did not hinder democracy develop in that country. In the American honesty to keep her promise of pull out from Iraq at the earliest, has anybody any doubt, while considering the precedents? All including the enemies know that this promise will be kept if there is any postponement, that will only be for a short while for organisational and strategic reasons. It is the vigilant American public opinion which is taking care of these promises. But what is the aim of the opponents–especially the media and the terrorists? Their interest is to proclaim to the world that the US invasion of Iraq was a foolhardy idea, contrary to law and which produced only misery to the conquered. The media seems to have not only a vested interest but a permanent interest also in accusing and torpedoing Anglo–American schemes for normalisation. What after all is reconstruction? It is the inevitable consequence of war and its destruction. In order to complete the liberation war, the establishment of a legitimate government, preferably democratic shall be a decisive step. But a working state machine cannot be established in a country where there is no law and order. The pre-requisite for an orderly existence is to keep away hunger, want and misery through emergency economic aid. Americans are doing it in Iraq. In the liberated areas, law and order is better now. The food situation is satisfactory and there are no famine deaths.

The medical facility is improving and communications are restored and improved. Students go to school and ladies shop in bazaars. But these improvements, are hated and feared by a small number of people whose motives are political and their ambition is seizure of power by back-door. They are not the majority, but are only a handful, and this terrorizing minority is behind the hate campaign. They want to establish and proclaim that the American invasion of Iraq is no liberation at all, and it is only an attempt to destroy a great civilisation and religion–a modern day crusade by the Christian West to reconquer the sacred land. Regrettably the enemies of democracy include not only Arabs and Muslim fundamentalists, but the tabloid media also. The American media is especially allergic to the Bush administration making any significant contribution to world democracy and Human Rights. The media lambasts against prisoner abuse question. True, prisoner abuse is not condusive to the rules of democracy and Geneva Conventions. But is anybody fool-hardy enough to say that in the battle-field, a prisoner can be dealt with as decently as in a civil society? Maintaining and safe–guarding prisoners, is a real extension of the battle-field, and this job is entrusted not to civilians but to the military itself. In the war front, if some errors and defaults and abuses happen, that is an ordinary happening though not permitted. It is the generality of military behaviour that is to be considered and not isolated incidents. There is no allegation, as in the case of Cossacks in the Second World War, that mass murder of innocent prisoners have been perpetrated in prisons by American soldiers on the basis of deliberate conspiracy and design in the military. If the American prison authorities are doing interrogation according to civil law, will it produce any result? An interrogation is likely to run into rough methods, and that is inescapable if they want results. Usually prison scenes are never shown outside. It is common knowledge that even if the normal details of prison conduct are told out, it will look disgusting. A repulsive and defaming prison abuse could be denied in the past, as merely wordy reportage, but now because of recorded visions it becomes impossible to deny. But petty human rights violations are not viewed with concern in the battlefield, where the bloody trade of death and destruction shadow and belittle these newsworthy violations. There is the law against thefts, but still thefts do take place. When a prisoner is caught, disarmed and disciplined, in the same process he will be forced, humiliated and threatened, and again he is cajoled, praised and proffered too for disclosing war details. If the people of the world happen to see the video shots of the full action of capture and imprisonment of prisoners of war (POW) that will invariably involve a lot of bad scenes repugnant to civil order and amounting to human rights violations, and violation of Geneva conventions. Now the American people may remember what Lincoln said during the civil war "When arms clash, the law falls to the ground" and he said those words as rebuff to the confrontationist—Chief Justice Taney, and his Habeas Corpus writs. Every prisoner of war is expected to carry some information regarding war secrets, and he will give out this information only in coercive, compelling and threatening circumstances. Can the military authorities say that they will be satisfied with whatever information they get through civilian law questioning only when information comes crucial for future military moves? These military interrogations will become a useless, purposeless act as no prisoner will speak anything important in decent civil questions carried on under the rigour of the fifth amendment. We have to shudder at the thought of stopping the questioning of POW which means that even at the cost of losing the war, the military has to be civilised. Then we will save the liberty of the enemy and endanger our own liberty. What is the motive of the media in blowing the petty defaults of war, out of proportion? They never care that the country's honour and safety depends on winning the war and not losing it. They never care that their own safety and security are also bound up with the safety and security of their own free political system and it never depends on the victory of the enemy. True, the media man does not use guns and bombs to sabotage his country 's interests, but they employ their pen to weaken and damage the war effort of their own country with devastating consequence to their freedom. The media forced the US to surrender in Vietnam, and in that case the Congress was playing exactly to the media tune and what was the result? Came the most nasty and humiliating surrender in American history, in spite of the fact that on the day of Vietnam surrender, America had enough arms to win many world wars. What America missed was war leadership and weak leadership was laid siege by the hunting media. This was what happened in France in 1939. All important French newspaper editors and owners were bribed by Hitler, and the result was the call by the French press not to go to war against the invincible German columns; whereas it was really the French defence forces which were invincible in the early stages of the war especially from 1935 to 1938. But the corrupt, tabloid antinational media played havoc and the crime of the press came to light very late. Whether the proponents of Watergate were bribed by communist countries has never been investigated but there was strong suspicion that they were working to the full advantage of the enemy. When Richard Nixon resigned, the media was exultant; when Vietnam fell to Communists, they were more exultant. In the Indian case of Tehelka, the treason committed by the Tehelka has been covered up and whitewashed by sensational tabloidisation. Military secrets are stolen, and military installation are bugged and forcible entry made. Such seditious acts are to be tried by military courts but the poor democracy tolerates all these crimes. These upstarts succeed in destabilising democracy, throughout the world, but to our surprise they go unpunished. Democracy never got her full benefits of democratisation, only because of the media man she herself begot and reared. He is always criticising and condemning her veracity, capacity and credibility, and all this damage done often by blatant lies and misrepresentation. The world shall think how to control this knowledge industry which seldom is disseminating knowledge, but manufactures it in large quantities and corrupt it. The press came into existence only as the defender and spokesman of human rights and the free government protecting these rights, but now the media is set on a course deleterious to these rights.

The search by Anglo-British team for WMD in Iraq reached nowhere, and now the search by the western media continues vigorously to prove that Saddam was unarmed when he was overthrown. The media has a deep interest in not discovering any WMD, and thereby accuse the Anglo-American authorities of pre-meditated and prejudicial motives against Saddam. Is WMD the only reason for attacking Iraq? Is, the discovery of WMD having any conclusive bearing or detrimental effect on the motives of war? That Iraq was ruled by an in-human dictator is true. He committed genocidal crimes as institutional, and he never hides his intention and preparations to eliminate enemies–both real and imaginary. His anti-people crimes and mass murders continued. He killed thousands of Kurds by pumping in poison gas. After the First Gulf War and on his restoration, quite contrary to Geneva Conventions, the revolters were identified and shot as collaborators. The regime of mass murder and repression has been re-established with a vengeance and the voracious slaughter engine restored. This murderous regime continued for more than a quarter century. Genocides, never get a peoples' mandate. This dictator went to war with Iran on the charge that the latter was planning his overthrow. But the ten-year war was a calamity for both. The threat to world peace unfolded in naked shape when Iraq attacked Kuwait in 1990 on the lame excuse that Kuwait is secretly draining away Iraqi underground oil. In the face of very powerful military powers like the United States, Britain, Germany, France, Japan, Soviet Union and China, Saddam is attempting his conquests with smaller forces, but the surprise is that none came forward to stop him before starting. He violated international law and broke all international conventions in demonstrated contempt. In the midst of this multiple crime complex, the media and the critics are moving heaven and earth to disprove that WMD was stored in Iraq in large quantities. Saddam once made it and used it to kill thousands of humans, and the world witnessed it with horror and grief. Given the means, he can make these products in no time, and repeat his crimes against humanity many times. But to give court like proof to the world-media, is not possible. But the media contends that unless Saddam is sitting on storage tanks filled with poison gas with standby launching machines, there is absolutely no justification for Bush Jr. to go to war. The media is eagerly contending that the person who committed a million murders did not certainly commit the offence of burglary. When we look at BBC newscasts, we are forced to believe that the weapons of mass destruction (WMD) are a bogey, and this state run news organisation is out to destroy the efforts or America and Britain to restore law and order in Iraq. The first priority is that there has to be an elected government in Iraq where elected governments are viewed with enmity, derision and contempt by all absolutist regimes around. The countries that support US military intervention in Iraq are now concerned of the future repercussions of the founding of a free regime in Baghdad. So the terror attacks are continuing and difficult to track the source. And terrorists are favoured by all kings and dictators in the middle east.

17
The World Enquires Into The Morals Of The Iraq War

Is the media committed to the cause of the free society and human rights? But the conduct of the media declares that they are anti-human rights, anti-freedom and they are never in favour of peoples' rights. The photos of human rights violations committed in the US military camps in Iraq are leaked out, printed and telecast to the world as if it is a military operation to surprise the enemy. But compare these photos with the torture sessions and the shooting and hanging sprees committed by Saddam and his henchmen? Are these photo exhibits by the media leading to the democratization of Iraq or its terrorisation and disintegration? Media can get many dirty things to publish, but should they publish it all? The world knows that India is a fully free democracy where human rights are well protected according to international standards. But visit any police station in the country without warning and you can see Iraqi like figures in many police stations across this free democracy. Not that such abuses are not taking place in other countries as well, but such abuses are published to the world by the media only in a selective way. When we see the scene of a mass murder or tragedy we take our eyes away; but when we see the picture of a naked man taunted in a police station or a lady caught by her skirt on the road, we attentively look and stare. But the first case is violation of a basic rights and natural rights of man, which is abhorrent. The second is only violation of decency. But because of media tabloidisation the people are compelled to look to the second offence only.

This media concern with petty human rights is telling on their credibility. It is well demonstrated that the media does not want the attempt to democratise Iraq succeed. They hope the reconstruction of Iraq also shall not succeed. They want to condemn the free world and they want the free world dishonoured. The big question to be asked by a responsible mediaman about Iraq shall be the prospect of establishing a democratic regime and the reconstruction of the country. Iraq on reconstruction can be a very prosperous country with petro dollars. In the democractisation process the great hurdle is the media hostility towards that programme, and not improbable that the media has been bribed to sabotage the process of democratisation by these terrorist forces. So they invent episodes and seize any dirty opportunity to play dirty tricks. They completely blacked out the news on reconstruction. When there is food scarcity, they shoot and publish those pictures of human want, but when food supply is plenty and the hospitals are working smooth, they black out those scenes. Having no interest in Iraqi reconstruction, it appears that the media campaign has been supported by terrorists to toe their line, or they are threatened to toe their line. The world will never know these secret deals. It is not a handful of petty human rights violations which are important in the case of Iraqi people. It is their date with democracy and reconstruction which should be handled first. But as the American president election is fast approaching, the media is moving high and low to prevent the re-election of George W. Bush-who is not conforming to their choice of mediocrity. Bush is a strong president and all strong rulers in democracy are condemned and defiled by the media for invented crimes, and such condemnations lead only to tragic results for democracy. When a Vietnamese monk committed self-immolation in Saigon, the world press carried it in banner headlines. But when finally America chose to surrender they called it a human tragedy, unimaginable and unprecedented. More than a million fleeing the communist terror drowned in the South China Sea–and another million fled to other shores where they were unwelcome. The persecution of the erstwhile South Vietnamese was making that country into a holocaust camp, in the immediate aftermath of the war. On these sufferings what was the response of the then-media.

There were reports that the campus revolts and the Watergate armageddon were the result of funding by communist international, but then who cares for an independent investigation of these treason charges! All they wanted was to depose a very able defender of American democracy–Richard Nixon. The congressional hostility towards the president was reaching murderous manifestations and nobody bothers if the honour and strength of American democracy is being damaged and disfigured in the process. There is a lot of media mischief directly telling on the stability and growth of democracy in the world, and this mischief-making has become their basic right now almost constitutionalised. The media wants only democracy's interest harmed and jeopardised, but they fail to recognise that they exist only with democracy and they are the by product of that system. In world democracies there happen violations of human rights, but there is no genocide in a democracy much less there are holocausts and mass tortures. It is desirable that all the rights defaults are avoided, prevented and eliminated and the attempt shall go on. But there is no system of government, where all rights are always protected without default; and democracy also is no exception. It is widely recognised that no system allows as much protection to human rights as democracy allows, and in this respect there is no fourth estate and media man without democracy. But in practice the media serves only the case of inhuman administrations and this may not lie intentional but the result of their conduct. I am yet to hear a good word from a journalist that democracy alone provide maximum protection to human rights and liberty. But democracy baiting is the one and only motive and function of the journalist hunt for sinners, and they dangerously jeopardise the interests of the free world. Never we heard that the journalist has jeopardized and destroyed the interests of a dictator. Could they do any harm to dictator Saddam Hussein when he committed thousands of murders in Iraq. The journalist knows that by attacking the politics and polices of Saddam, they may invite only vengeful retaliation. They know also that there is absolutely no use in the criticism of a dictator because a dictator never cares for popular opinion, much less press comments. One will wonder why rare references are made by the press on the Tiananmen Square incident of 1989, in which more than a thousand students were crushed to death by Chinese tank columns. The condemnation of Tiananmen incident comes mainly from democratic leaders and rarely from the press. We find it hard why the press is unconcerned about the murderous crimes of dictators and tyrants, whereas they pounce on the petty, white collar crimes and statutory crimes of democracy. They cry against a petty burglary, but a murder is uncommented. Why the media assume this anti-people role ? There are two reasons. Their opinion are valid only in democracies; secondly they are incapable of influencing the acts of tyrants. The result is that journalists often become the undeclared enemy of leading democracies of the world—a consequence unimagined by the protagonists and partisans of the Fourth Estate.

In the aftermath of the Second Gulf War, the wholesale energy of the journalist and the electronic media were focussed on attacking the mysterious aims and motives of George W. Bush in going for war. The world saw many historic wars and battles in which one side wins and the other side loses. It is the winner who determines the principles and morals of war with retrospective validity but though ridiculous, such validation is accepted by history but the media never enters into a futile enquiry on the motives of the opponents and the motives of a war already waged. In real terms the side quite sure of victory wanted to go for war to make an easy win, and nothing satisfies a statesman like a war and victory, whereas the other side wants to avoid the war only because he is not sure of the capacity of his army and his capacity to win. A post-mortem examination of the causes of the First World War is still going on and the researchers digging deeper into the war archives are unimpressed of the causes already discovered. The motives of Kaizer Whilhem II, his confidence in the superiority of the German army, its valour and strategy are cited as the motive forces for igniting the power keg. Once the war starts, it sucks in the forces around it into the vortex, and then the partners are mere victims moving with the torrent and terror of the war. This may be good game for the student and historian to delve deep and extricate mysterious reasons, but the fact is that some decisive voice at the fateful moment decided to cast his lot for battle, unmindful of the consequences, and his subsequent inability to stop the shooting war that escalated into unimagined shapes.

Iraq can be a just cause for America to defend. But is it possible to defend all just causes? It is only rarely that just causes find good defenders. The world can know that China's human rights record makes a good cause for outside intervention especially when 1300 million people are kept as government hostages and the people enjoy only bits of economic freedom. For a while the people are dazzled by the fast growing economy which brings in many new comforts for the hitherto deprived. When you make material and economic gains, you may be better inclined to sacrifice a bit of your human rights for the sake of consumptive comfort, and in what way China, gives her people a case for good economic choices. But still there will be a strong desire for freedom, and a fast building resentment against autocracy, whether it is personal despotism or totalitarianism. I say, if the American rationale is invoked, there is a very good case for liberating Chinese people by outside forces. But will any one attempt it? If not what is the reason? China is already a big power and a substantive nuclear power, also, and any liberation war may invite a nuclear response which will be disastrous for both contenders. In that war, instead of a country full of liberated people, there will be a land full of dead bodies, and such a destination to mass funeral is tragic. When Russia invaded Hungary to suppress the rebellion against communist rule, there existed an emphatic and just case for an Iraq-like liberation. But no big power, let alone USA, was prepared to intervene because such intervention would lead to a direct conformation with Soviet Union, and to nuclear war. We do not want the earth blasted out and dead, but we want it alive. So all just causes are not causes for war. In any just case like Tiananmen or Budapest or the East German uprising of 1954, or the Berlin Blockade of 1948, any intervention was absolutely justifiable, but no intervention happened. War occurs not because there exists a just cause for it, but because the war-makers think it feasible, desirable, and convenient in the existing circumstances. Then why the media enquiry or the moralist's enquiry for finding out the just cause or causes that existed to justify the invasion of Iraq? America felt that she could afford to invade Iraq and overthrow Saddam, the most maligned dictator alive. Wars turn out inconvenient on most occasions, and now George W. Bush is facing a media trial whether he can present the political morals to convince the American people to vote for him once more. The experience is that when a leader was at war, he is assured of certain re-election, and this was the case regarding Wilson, FD Roosevelt and Truman. Now there comes a different situation. The people of America are sure that Bush Jr. has won the Iraq war, Saddam thrown out and proposed for trial, and Bush is going to finish the job, which his father has left unfinished. However, the present day American democracy is not the courageous one we saw during the Second World War. Post War America is fickle and media governed. The media contends that Americans are still dying in Iraqi terror and this is due to Bush foolishly going to challenge the Muslim fundamentalists. Congress and the media are very busy thinking of how to defeat George W. Bush in the next election in November 2004. It is a reflection on American democracy that a strong and capable President has been hampered in his bold mission of liberation by adverse media trial. Though Bush went to war in Iraq and Afghanistan for liberating the people, and the majority feels that the ultimate liberation has been accomplished, the jealous media misrepresents everything done to the honour of American greatness. They say the war has been won on wrong reasons. They will also discover that American soldiers are dying in small numbers even after the war is over. How meaningless, impractical, unreal representation of the causes and effects of war! What is inescapable in a war is death or rather martyrdom. Could anybody in history wage a war without soldiers and civilians dying? The media raises the most irresponsible argument, but still the people are misled. Such misrepresentations usually disable the war-effort leading to have the battle front discouraged, and in legal language this attempt is called treason. Simply because the media commits it, it is not untreasonable, as it is made to appear. Here the government should boldly prosecute those people whether Congressmen, media men or political opponents who deliberately and intentionally sabotage the engine of war. Nevertheless, any ruling politician is afraid of these classes of detractors called media men. They continue to misrepresent and disable the country's capacity for war, but go unpunished.

A post-mortem examination of the intentions and motives of war is irrelevant considering the results and consequences of war. The one relevant question of history is whether the President has won the war or lost it. America conquered Iraq, deposed its ruler, captured him and they have appointed an interim government but not elected by the people. True this is a government picked up by occupiers only to serve interim. But the media say that the Americas intentions are not what is told out. The intentions are to be gathered from the causes and consequences of the act which the intention has provoked. Here America intended to attack Iraq, subjugate it and take it over. Conquered it is and taken over, and then what better intention on hideous intention they have to disclose? Bush won the war with the smallest number of casualities but the media says that Bush can go for war, but he has no right to shed American blood in the battlefield. A new question is to be asked – is America a nation fully afraid of war as claimed by the Congress and the media? Are Americans afraid of dying in battle?

18
The Impact Of Iraq War On Bush Re-election

People go to war because they find it in the great tradition; or because they find it convenient to do so. Also they go to war because of the compulsions of national honour. They go to defend another country, as Britain and France did in the beginning of the Second World War to defend Poland. Again, I may point out that wars come not to be waged on any deliberate design, but often by conceit and arrogance, and the reckless unreasonableness and suicidal rashness of any country, which fires the first shot. In the frightening atmosphere, all jump into the bloody fray and once the fight begins all are mere pawns in the chessboard of arms. Wars end in the complete defeat and surrender of the opponent. This happened in Iraq when the Saddam regime collapsed like a pack of cards and he went into hiding in the Second Gulf War. The world media are still unconvinced of the justness of the Bush motives, and so the present war between media and George W. Bush. The media accuse that Bush is amateuristic, unintelligent and foolhardy enough to jump into misadventures like Iraq and Afghan wars, and his re-election will send wrong signals to the free world on the morals of war, when morality makes a thunderous return. So, according to the new morals redrawn by the media, the real victory for America lies in the Bush defeat in the next election. This moral restructuring of war ethics brings in a new momentum and credibility for dictators, terrorists, abductors, car bombers and hijackers. The media defends this new class.

Saddam Hussein ruled Iraq for more than a quarter century and destroyed the social, economic and cultural fabric of that very ancient civilization. The first thing he did immediately after coming to power is executing the entire ruling class in one operation which left only one man among them alive-Saddam Hussein. So the political system has been abruptly decimated and he was the lone ruler controlling the Baath Party and government. He wanted to make Iraq the safest fortress for him to rule, and elimination after elimination followed and in the regime of purge even closest relations were not spared. Saddam belongs to the Sunny minority. The Shia majority was brutally suppressed and their voice ruthlessly muffled. He built many golden palaces for himself where he revelled. After establishing himself firmly in power, he went over to the mission of conquests. First he attacked Iran, and this war shattered his dreams and left his country bleeding and reeling. More than a million died in that atricidal war, but he was as remorseless as inhuman. His home adventures destroyed the country and economy and the people were in dire straits. The economy was bled white. He was unmoved and state terror and repression were unleashed to absolute unaccountability. The entire home opposition has been eliminated and the genocidal purge came to a full circle to deadly completion. No dissent surfaced and Saddam made sure of eliminating the last dissenting soul also. Then he takes the fateful decision in 1989 for building a new empire and this was by conquest of Kuwait. There is no stopping him, and the undefended Kuwait has been battered and subjugated within days, but the international responses were unexpectedly frightening to him. The American friendship and comraderie of the Iran-Iraq war days vanished in thin-air and a Western Coalition of Liberation immediately took shape. Under the half resolute Bush Sr. the Coalition forces marched into Kuwait, in Desert Storm and drove out the Iraqi marauders, and then they marched into Baghdad itself. When Saddam and his terror regime were about to collapse American defeatism once again raises its ugly head to overpower Bush Sr. under the moral compulsions of a United Nations Resolution.The President was advised to limit the war on Kuwait territory, as Iraqi territory was illegal area as per the resolution. Bush immediately orders to stop the raid and leave Saddam, alone and safe. The world was waiting without gasp to witness the overthrow and capture of Saddam, but they were shocked to see the American President making an unnecessary, uncalled for capitulation, in the hour of triumph. The President was a confused soul, and in him, the capitulative instinct ought to have been irresistible. There will be advisors, but it is for the president to decide and the President alone is held responsible for any decision, America felt defeated and humbled and the world stood surprised at the logic of a war and defeat and was wholly unprepared to digest this affront to history. The President brought defeat and dishonour in the splendid hour of glory, and there must be popular revenge.

For an incumbent President re-elections are not anxious occasions, unless it is a dismal show as in the case of Ford and Carter. However, in 1991 the people felt defamed and humbled and they will take revenge on their President. Revenge it was and in the President election of 1992, George H.W. Bush was voted out, and

America chose Bill Clinton. But 2003 and the Second Gulf War are different stories. In the place of father now the son is in the White House. In the 2003 Gulf war, the Anglo-American coalition has been deserted by the European Big Two–Germany and France, and international cooperation is as partial as discouraging. But the Bush-Blair team makes up the loss with determination and resolve, and launch the second invasion of Iraq. The much vaunted Republicans Guards of Saddam are nowhere, and his Iraqi regime collapsed in no time. After many months, Saddam is captured and he is now on the way to trial and punishment by an Iraqi Tribunal.

2004 AD also faces a new election, and American people go to polls in November to elect or unelect the complete conqueror of Iraq George W. Bush Jr. The history of Winston Churchill, but for whose leadership Britain would have lost the Second World War, stands in the way to caution. The glory of war and its victory does not guarantee election victory, though America hitherto did not fail to re-elect war winners like Wilson, FDR and Truman. Now there are upsetting changes in the political morals that sweep the American mind. The press, the Congress and the politician stood solidly behind Wilson, FDR, and Truman, but now they sympathise with Saddam Hussein and criminal terror. According to the emerging morals of the defeatist, the intelligentia, the think-tanks and congressional caucuses, war is illegal, victory is immoral, armed fights are cowardly and martyrdom simply political gimmick. Bush and Blair committed these crimes in large scale and then will the Americans vote for Bush Jr. in November 2004? When media builds up its institutional hostility and hatred towards strong political leadership–the chances of Bush Jr. looks dim. Unlike his father, Bush Jr. brought glory to America and this is the time for the people to thank him. However, how the American voter is going to react, remains a big question. Here the mysteries of democracy are perplexing to its interests, when it treats a winner with hatred and a loser with applause. When the free American cannot identify his enemies and friends, he runs into political wilderness.

Democracy can defend the peoples' rights, but cannot defend itself, and that is a dangerous practice of the present. The most powerful ruler of the world is still the President of the United States, but that strong man is weak in defending his person. In the midst of these confusing signals, it is a story in good luck that democracy survives. This story of mass appeal and mass approval of the merit of democracy looks vulnerable due to many reasons. The inherent strength of democracy is not force but only will, and this will the democratic leader often lacks, and his government is forced into failures. But surprise it is that when all other political and military forces collapse, with no defenders to protect, democracy emerges as the final option of the people. But democracy is safe only in those places where the supremacy of the civilian authority has become the basic creed and a way of life, as in United States, United Kingdom, Canada, Australia, India etc. In other places, democracy stands diffident and vulnerable to inimical forces. But the enemies are from within, and they are the leaders who lead it astray, the media who misinforms and its defenders who are non-committed or half-committed or cowardly. A degree of security has been reached only in those traditional democracies like the United States and United Kingdom.

The exigencies of democratic behaviour are making the life of democracy exposed to danger and this is what we face in the election of the most powerful ruler on earth–the President of the United States. A President who wins a war is not assured of re-election and a President who loses a war is not threatened with election defeat also. Cannot America distinguish between victory and defeat? Then why should a President of the United States win a war? In addition, why should the President move the heavens to avoid defeat in the battlefield? All are meaningless sweating and swerving, when it comes to war and peace. Bush Jr. is pleading for his re-election in November 2004, and strange that it is victories, that eclipse his electoral prospects. When the media and the congress lay siege to the White House, Bush is running for cover and he is desperately campaigning. Interesting it must be to find out why the President of the US is going desperate, after a victorious war. The world knows that when the American President is a loser, the free world is forced into insecurity. All rulers in democracy strive for success in the battlefield hoping that success always guarantees victory in the battle of ballots also. But the peoples' reactions are often self-contradictory and curious.

But for a President Election in November 2004, would Bush go for a premature, haphazard, and dangerous handover of power in Iraq! The media tutored the American people and these people warn the President that in battles no American shall die, but the war must be fought, but they don't care for victory. This is the terrible democratic formula for war. In spite of the advent of push button war machines, we are yet to come across a deathless war, though wars are undying. Wars are really mass funerals for a distant observer. More than half a million soldiers died in the American Civil War; in the two World Wars more than a hundred million died, and in the Korean War and the Vietnam war, hundreds of thousands again died. America lost the Vietnam War in spite of the American death toll rising to fifty five thousand. But all these American dead in the wars did not die in vain. Those dead really died to save the worlds democracies and to destroy anarchies and dictatorships. The Presidents who led the World Wars and the Korean War anyhow did not meet the dismal fate of Ford, Carter and Sr. Bush. President Wilson won his two terms and FD Roosevelt won his fourth term. In the case of FDR it was feared that the more he was war-time President, the more popular he became, and so dangerously unbeatable in polls, and FDR died in office. In those days, the American press stood fired with patriotism, and rallied behind their President. Then the national conscience of America was not marred and misled by misinformation. There were no wrong priorities for the media except the success of the nation in wars whether waged in the neighbourhood or abroad. But now what is the situation? The media never insist that America should win her wars, and George W. Bush openly complains that the media does not want victory in Iraq. They want to misinform that wars are anti-people and illegal, and it is in breach of international law. The media man does not care if American interests are sacrificed in the battlefield, bringing home dishonour. We are then forced to ask if the media has gone anti-national? The essential result of media discoveries in the United States and of late in Britain are to obstruct and discredit the war effort. I cite an example: In spite of all these technological and medical advances, people die in wars. There is death by protracted sufferings; death with agonising convulsions; death inch-by-inch and instant death. If a number of video shots of the convulsions and agonies are shown to the audience and if these injured are the victims of Anglo-American firepower, these scenes of human agony will leave a deep and adverse impression about the war crimes committed in Anglo-American battle practices. But these are only ordinary war scenes. But what the audience gets is a picture of American cruelty and dastardliness and the American voters are bound to react angrily in an immediate election. What is the truth? In every war, there will be indiscriminate deaths and destruction, which if witnessed live will be shocking to world conscience. But these are common happenings in the battle field. The opponents of the United States commit far worse crimes and cruelties but they turn a deaf ear to these dramatics of the tabloid media. The great victim of these media perversions is the misinformed common man in a democracy who votes against the incumbent President in disgust. Thus, the electorate shoots down a President in the midst of a resolute war prosecution, and what it supplies is delight and pleasure to the enemy. The enemy always wants a capable war leader to fail, as Hitler went into wild tantrums when he heard that FD Roosevelt died suddenly in New York just before the end of World War II. Wars are won not only by arms, but by leadership also, and the tragedies in Korea and Vietnam loudly proclaim this theory. The Iraqi insurgents are eager to see George W. Bush defeated in the November election, and they hope any other President will be friendly. Therefore, the November 2004 election also is a war against terror. Will America abide by the wishes of the enemy in the crossfire between Iraqo-philes and Iraqo-phobes in November 2004? It has become impossible to prosecute a war to victory, and this war may prolong for years, and some times surviving many President elections. It is not the courage, strategy and sacrifices of the soldier in battlefield, which matters with the voter. What works with the voter now are the seeds of misinformation sown by the unethical media running the game of lies, half-truths, and tabloids? They stand, often unintentionally, against the interests of the mother country. This media distraction is not a majoritarian revolution; and not being a majoritarian act, it is a challenge to the democratic principle that the majority's preferences shall prevail.

If President Bush is voted out, what will be the turn of events in the leadership of the world? John Kerry the opponent has no clear policy on Iraq and Afghanistan. But sensing the wind, he is always blowing hot and cold without hesitation. Policy-less, he is engaged in the aimless rhetoric of waffling, evasion, escapism and confusion, and what he profess is a policy of 'no policy'. Only till George W. Bush is in office, Kerry can criticise Bush on Iraq, but he is unable to outline what his policy will be in Iraq. Saying that his policy is a high secrecy, is really committing fraud on the people. He leaves the voter simply to speculate. If people vote for a no policy, that is a vote for anything Kerry wants to do, and people usually do not vote for blank policies. Kerry attacks that Bush went to war and exposed America to dangers and this war is unnecessary. War is always dangerous but when war comes, you have to fight and win it, if you want to survive. Those unwilling to court danger, are exposing America to the dangers of defeat and humiliation. By crushing the terrorists in Afghanistan and Iraq, is not America becoming safer? Truman was battling the far away Korea to make America safe and world democracy safer, and America had to fight her great wars far-away from her territory's borders. General Eisenhower, before his swearing in, was finding fault with all that Truman did in Korea though, Truman was not then Eisenhower's election opponent. Eisenhower was elected, and the world expected that he will write in Korea a new chapter in courage and adventure and will corner the aggressor and punish him. But the new President, except his election rhetorics, had no scheme either to win or lose the war, and things moved into stalemate. He had no clear programmes for Korea, and confusion prevailed. The great general will fight only if told by his political boss. He cannot command but only obey the politician's commands. This great commander of World War II became the irresolute, aimless chief executive of the US. His promises in the Korea to roll back communism in Asia and Europe turned out mere political fiction, and Truman later condemned that the Korean armistice was a sell out. It was North Korea who unleashed a naked aggression on South Korea, and this was part of the communist expansion scheme in East Asia. Korea was a trial balloon hoisted by China to test the mettle of the new United States policy of containment under that brinkman and cold warrior-called John Foster Dulles. It was really American bluff which Red China called Red China evolved her grand strategy to conquer more and some conquests were cleverly concealed as border wars and disputed territory, and this euphemism worked to her fantastic advantage. To have critics are of no use, unless they have a policy and action plan. It is only in the Democratic Convention that Kerry admits that going to Iraq has been a proper American response and he supports it. But again he will add that Bush has exposed America to unnecessary dangers-but he fails to explain what are they and how are they. Kerry lacks the will and is shying away from details. A presidential candidate should place a different policy and strategy before the people-but Kerry has only criticism. Eisenhower had only criticism to offer and he had no policy and strategy for Korea to unfold before the American electorate-and this led to a sell out of American interests. The Korean debacle was followed by the Indo-China War and the French withdrawal, sending clear signals on what Red China plans to do in future. America was hesitating and then retreating. For the United States, not to have aided the French in the Indo-China war, was a disastrous mistake. If the French had given a tough fight, there would have been no Vietnam War of 1963-1975 and mass tragedy and rout for America. Only Mc. Arthur visioned the writings on the wall. He pleaded with the United States leadership to wage an all out war against China on Korea, and he emphasised that even at the risk of a powerful Red-China challenging the United States for an all out war, it shall be fought. However, neither Truman nor his successor Eisenhower accepted a programme for total war, and China emerged triumphant to make more challenges. Naked conquests were renamed as guerrilla wars and liberation wars, and in every case America was struggling her best to surrender to the enemy and surrenders became the ultimate American strategy in Asia. Will it be her strategy in Iraq also?

19
America – The Nuclear Monopolist Refused To Go Conquering

A kind of defeatism has gripped and over-powered the American conscience accelerating towards comfort-living, and in that consumerist milieu, they lost their self-respect and honour. Now a consumer society has replaced the courageous society of the American revolution that inspired the French Revolution. What America wants today are the comforts of affluence, and that is actively reflected in congressional attitudes. At present even the ordinary pursuits of a nation so powerful as America can mount world revolutions. American military might may still be able to conquer the world without damage to her homeland, and America can change into the ruler of the world, only if she sheds her defeatism, consumerism and isolationism. It is only by going to war that America becomes safer, and not by running away, Wars are to make the country stronger, and thereby safer, but Kerry says the Iraq War made America unsafe. This declaration frightens the fearfuls among Americans, and lecturing on the art of fear shall not be the business of a political leader. Kerry should make America not fearful but courageous.It is not docility but adventures that made her a great nation. An American ruler must know that the economic and military might of America continues over-whelmingly superior and therefore any American military programme in the 21st century is not exposing her to dangers. A future American President, unknowing this power, is a real danger to the nation. Because of the collapse of the Soviet Union and demise of Cold War, America enjoys today a safety and superiority, which is unprecedented. In the midst of that glory, should America surrender in Iraq as they did in Korea and Vietnam? Kerry saying that by going to war in Iraq-where the fight has been ridiculously unilateral in favour of Coalition. America has become dangerously unsafe is a clear misrepresentation, insulting the American defence forces. Kerry is making calls only to American cowardice and not to her heroism and this national disgrace America should emphatically disown. These are Kerry insinuations on America, Kerry can be better than Bush only if the former unfolds a more adventurous Middle East Policy to contain terrorists, and till now he has none.

In 1945, America was having the monopoly of nuclear arms and this unique advantage continued till 1949, when Russia exploded her first bomb. If, instead of Truman, it were Stalin, Tojo, Hitler, or Mussolini who got it first, they certainly would have issued immediate ultimatums to the whole world to surrender. This will be a terrible call for armageddon or more clearly a call for the next World War which sometimes may convert into a global counter-revolution. Hitler or Stalin acquiring the first bomb, these tyrants brandishing the bomb before the world, would have never hesitated to ask the world leaders to come and surrender at Berlin or Moscow, at once. The people of the world reading the history of 1945-1949 should make no mistake about this scenario. Hitler always wanted an atom bomb, and he even boasted of the final weapon to win and this was the atom bomb. However, he was unlucky to halt his bomb project midway as there were conscientious objectors among his scientists in committing a million murders in one strike. Reading through the message of communism for a world revolution without territorial boundaries, also reinforces this possibility as their ideological scheme and demand, before the state withers away. With the first bomb in hand, Stalin would have theorised it also as the inevitable invention of World Marxism, under proletarian dictatorship. But Stalin or Hitler or Mussolini did not get this opportunity to conquer the whole world by a single decree-that opportunity came only to Harry, S. Truman, and Truman failed even to imagine that way. What option will the countries of the world have, when the destruction and death caused at Hiroshima and Nagasaki looks so horrible and tragic to their naked eye? Whatever may be the quantity of conventional weapons, it is no match for the whopping destruction to be caused to man and civilisation by the nuclear bomb. Then who tied the hands of Truman back? It is the American public opinion, its discipline and its morals. American democracy or any other democracy is permanently unready for conquests. Here we exclude pseudo democrats and demagogues. Americans will invade, but will not subjugate and that is their 20th century practice. This democratic conscience of American war policy is so transparent as to disable it at every spearhead of fighting for conquest and annexation.They conquered Japan and liberated it; they conquered Philippines only to grant her independence; they conquered Western Europe and liberated it; they took over Panama, built the canal and left it free; they reconquered South Korea and liberated it. But she had historic failures too in this respect. The whole territory occupied by Allies and the territory of Russia and the Russian occupied lands in the Second World War could have been converted into freedom, if FDR and Truman pursued a bolder policy at Yalta and Postdam. There they bargained the least. In dividing the spoils of war, America was wrongly magnanimous. When the Second World War ended, America, with her nuclear monopoly, could have forced even Russia to grant freedom to the Russian people themselves, and liberated them, but American democracy is unadventurous. Eastern Europe could have been brought under self-rule and democracy, but America committed a serious failure of duty on Eastern Europe. If America aggressively pursued this course during 1945-48, the world's terror regimes in Russia and Eastern Europe could have been liquidated at one stroke of Truman's pen, and that would have remained the greatest liberation movement in history. If that happened, a communist China would never have been born. But a massive liberation movement must be backed by adventurous decisions. This the communist world had while the United States did not, much less other democracies, and this democratic passivity resulted in the loss of Eastern Europe and even Russia to communism. No country except the United States, will allow an inferior power to win, and dominate her in an act of political magnanimity. India showed this magnanimity towards Bangladesh during the war of liberation in 1971.

Wars are hated by democracy, and living dangerous is unpopular amongst the masses.In the usual course, the reign of democracy are in the hands of a majority, and majorities are always uncourageous, unadventurous, comfort-loving and therefore isolationist. Majorities hate war because it is risky and dangerous and that fear is sought to be covered up under some ideal and political principle, and they advocate retreat. Majorities had never been revolutionaries, and all revolutions in history are planned, organised and executed by determined and disciplined minorities, let it be French Revolution, American War of Independence, Russian Revolution or the Chinese Revolution. Revolutions are always mounted by regimented, disciplined bodies. Mostly Parisians carried out the French Revolution, and the French country-side only followed that lead, long after. Parisians were not a disciplined force. The Russian revolutionaries of Lenin were a notoriously small band of terrorists, but ready to shoot and kill. The men of Mao Tse Tung who captured power in China in 1949, were armed soldiers and they never had been a majority of Chinese. Here the minority could terrorise the majority into submission, only because the minority was organised and the majority remaining a mob. The mob has no general intent, and even in crisis cases too, the mob remains aimless, undisciplined and therefore powerless. So no wonder, even if Truman came forward to give an ultimatum to the communist world to surrender, the American Congress would immediately pass a resolution favouring the building of Iron Curtain. Such Truman ultimatum the American media would cry-down as neo-imperialism, ignoring the fact that in communist countries there is only deadly persecution and suppression of human rights. It is true that a revolution which ought to have happened in 1945 was postponed to 1989, only when the impenetrable, Iron Curtain rusted, corroded and collapsed. How much human suffering would have been saved, if America took the decisive step in 1945 when the physical power of the world stood bowing before her. Democracy talks too much but does little. Where she ought be bold, she comes apologetic.

Whether it is Afghanistan, or Iraq or Cuba or East Germany or Berlin or Vietnam, the American hesitancy and retreat caused her proteges to surrender and perish. Truman blurted out later that Eisenhower went to Korea and surrendered. Not only that; Eisenhower surrendered in East Germany, Hungary and in French Indo-China also. In French Indo-China he had no imaginative action plan to contain the future invasions of China and North Vietnam. The French, many years later, will reflect that given some American air support to them in Indo-China, they would have worked wonders, and there would have been a different story at Dien-Bien-Phu. If Dulles and Eisenhower had shown the courage to send troops and arms to Indo-China to relieve the trapped French garrison, there would have been no Vietnam War, which ended in disaster for USA in 1975. Any help to the French would have made America and South Vietnam safer. May be, there would have come a negotiated settlement, in which the communist domination would have been far less powerful. In the Chinese Civil War, America hesitated to give full support to Chiang on the reason that his army was inefficient and corrupt, and this critical stand denying the means of war to Chiang caused the greatest humiliation for America in Asia, and this was loss of China to Communism. Even after this madding shock, America never made an attempt to make a courageous stand in the subsequent theatres of conflict with communism, and the enemy was certain that America will leave Vietnam after some hesitant fights, and they called these American bluffs. After the loss of China, came Korea, and after fighting a long and costly war for three years, America failed to punish the main culprit – Communist China. It is true that South Korea has been recaptured but for the conqueror, this was again the triumphant homecoming unpunished and victorious. Because of these wars the Chinese fighting capacity was never dented and damaged, and that there will be more invasions was the clear message of Korea. The Indo-China war against the French started much before the Korean War, but the Chinese fighting qualities, exemplified in the Korean theatres, gave a new impetus to that ongoing war. From China and Russia, men and materials poured into Indo-China to assist the Ho chi-Minh forces. The drive could have been blunted with prompt American aid to the French, but Eisenhower and Dulles vacillated and then retreated and the French were abandoned by that powerful ally. As it is today, in 1954 also, the ultimate hope of the French depended on American help, but America refused help in any manner, and the vaunted American invincibility turned out a mirage. Fighter planes and helicopters were denied, and in the face of the increasing power and arms of the communist block in South East Asia, the French defeat became inevitable. True French decolonisation could not have been postponed for long, but effective American intervention would have prevented a communist take over, and the whole people being fed into that whopping grinder of red-rule. America may have desired to liberate Indo-China from French rule but to liberate in the Vietcong, way was to be swallowed up by China or North Vietnam, giving no place for the voice of the people. This is not liberation but enslavement. Decolonisation was followed by recolonisation by North Vietnam, and South Vietnam disappeared from the map. Strange that American help came always, but it was too little and often too late. America always hesitates, but never refuses to come; when she came limping all along suffering the assaults of the Congress and the media, we find the Congress jealous of any American victory abroad. The media thinks that any victory is a victory for the President with whom it is at war, and this is not a sweeping statement of fancy. Take any war or the civil wars in Indo-China, and examine the role played by the media, and the Congress. We see no news paper in America pleading to fight a war up to victory, let it be Vietnam, Korea, Laos, Angola, Cuba or the many civil wars in Eastern Europe, or the East German uprisings or, Gulf Wars. All the pleas of the media are focused in criticizing the actions of the free-world, and these assaults working as brake on the democratic locomotive going uphill. The media always highlights and condemns even the silly mistakes committed by the free world in the battle field, and they did only this way on any war America has waged.

20
Journalist Posted On The Political Left?

Though inconvenient the leftist media may answer these. Do they approve of the murders and persecutions committed by Saddam Hussein? Do they justify the invasion of Kuwait by Saddam? If they do not, have they ever pleaded that Kuwait shall be liberated by force? Do they believe that the aggression committed by North Vietnam on the South was liberation and whether communist liberation wars were really liberation of people to liberty? Do they believe that the mass-killings of one and half million innocents in Cambodia by Pol Pot in social engineering was a revolution or a grizzly slaughter? Do they believe that the North Vietnamese invasion of the South was a liberation war as the communists claim? Will they say that the killing of more than one thousand students at Tiananmen Square in Peking was not suppression of freedom of expression and violation of human rights? Will they answer why the totalitarian governments of Eastern Europe and Russia were overthrown by the people in a mass uprising in 1989? Why no communist country could ever reach the level of prosperity attained by the free world? Could the communists ever equal the technological excellence of the free world? Has the media ever supported a war in defence of human freedom and why they fail to defend the right of the free world? Have not the media deliberately as well as unwittingly played into the hands of communists, and helped the enslavement of people? Against tyrants like Mao Tse Tung, Fidel Castro, Causescue, Pol Pot and even Ho Chi Minh and the communist emperor Kim Ill Sung, have they moved a single finger when abominable crimes were perpetrated by them? The media have quite dubiously confined their war against the petty indiscretions of democracy, but ignoring the dangers it causes to democracy. The terror machines of dictators, pseudo-revolutionaries, tyrants and communists they have white washed–Why? Because dictators and terrorists are incorrigible first, and any criticism is a waste; secondly they retaliate in the violent way, even against media persons, whereas the boldest rebuke or retaliation they receive from a democrat may be as harmless a weapon as criminal prosecution in a court of law. A dictator or his henchman seldom hesitate fighting the media, even through personal attacks, but a democrat is rarely thinking that way. So the clever man that the media man is, he chooses democracy and her offspring as the perpetual media game, and in the remorseless witch-hunt, the same democracy that begot and reared him into a hit man, itself is chosen by him as target. This is sheer quirk of fate and a self contradiction in the media ethics on the question of human rights.

It is stranger how media man has metamorphosed into a committed foe of democracy, dangerously vindictive uncompromising and diabolic. It is politically judged that the most feared investigative journalist is the more than usual appendage of the political left, and they are directed to prey on the political right.

21
Responses Of The Courageous Vs The Cowardly

George W. Bush committing unprovoked aggression in Afghanistan and Iraq is an international criminal, and that is the latest argument of terrorists but not their last argument. Such all pervasive accusations can be made against any warring statesman It can be a conceited invader committing naked aggression or a patriot defending his country and going on the offensive. Such arguments cause a just a cover for inhuman sinners also. Can a legalist say that human wrongs can be confined to the narrow limits of state boundaries? If the law says so what is the basis for the existence of the United Nations and what is the relevance of the Universal Declaration of Human Rights? The world changes its thinking on global scales, and the compelling need of the times is to transfer all human interests into global case—dimensions. Every Human Rights violation is today a universal question as well as a local and state question. But this moral certainty is still awaiting the approval of international law, but international law, not having the sanction of force, lacks credibility. True, this difference in effectiveness is always there recognised, but it is international law that is gaining dominance over national law, and its practical side on human development shall not be ignored. In the earlier world or even in the immediate post-War World, there was no offence called crime against humanity, and this is internationalisation of what hitherto was considered pure domestic law. When international crime is an offence under international law, new problems in definition as well as in day to day use creates difficulties in giving practical application to lofty theories. Nationalism's conflict with internationalism, and similar questions, are innumerable and innovative.There is the International Court of Justice at Hague whose decrees are more violated than observed, like the new ruling of the court on the new 'Berlin wall' between Israel and Gaza. International law anyhow is making much headway, and its progression becomes irresistible in view of the favourable opinion existing at present. The former Yugoslav President-Slobodan Milosevic is standing trial in the new international criminal court at Hague, and this is a new offspring of International law. He is charged for crimes against humanity. In the trial, that court is following the rule of fair trial followed in a democracy, where rule of law is in force. Considering the problems of law that may arise in future on the question of possible. Bush outrages in Iraq, a case for war crimes can sometimes be brought against George W. Bush also. But the main question is what is the motive of Bush in toppling the Iraqi regime of Saddam, and what was the motive of Milosevic in his ethnic cleansing programme in the erstwhile Yugoslavia.

Like the Afghan war, the Iraq war also ended in American victory, and this victory stands against the practice of finding war criminals and crimes, only from among the losers and never from the winners. The Nazis were defeated, and so German State was found the criminal state. Japan was defeated and the Japanese warlords were found war criminals. War crimes are inseparably bound up with the question of victory and defeat. The winner becomes the prosecutor and judge and the loser the defendant. The principle that the winner be the prosecutor, and the vanquished the defendant, and the Judge an independent and impartial umpire are all rejected by war councils. If Germany had won the war, the war crimes tribunal would most probably been in London, and Churchill, Atlee, Eden, General Wavell, Montgomery, Mountbatten etc. would have been the criminals in the dock. Wars possess the indefeasible logic of giving the monopoly of justice to the winner, and the monopoly of crimes to the vanquished. In Iraq and Afghanistan–the victor is the Anglo-American Coalition and they got the monopoly of justice. The War Crimes Tribunal, in Iraq, unlike the Nuremberg Tribunal in Germany, is now designed as a domestic body composed of Iraqi citizens-who are asked to sit in judgment of their ex-ruler–Saddam Hussein. Sceptics were anxious that Saddam will be handed over to an absolute Iraqi custody. If there arise the possibility of a Saddam escape by defying custody and the law, a Bush victory in the November 2004 poll will be in jeopardy. But the Anglo-American powers decided to hand over Saddam to the custody of the Interim Governing Council headed by Allawi. It is doubted that America is holding Saddam in actual custody. The Governing Council composed of the arch-rivals of Saddam may give partial guarantee that Saddam will not find an easy escape or an easy excuse to go into hiding, once again. But Iraqi sovereignty is said to be already handed over back to Iraqis, and so any Saddam trial is presumed to be a domestic trial under Iraqi law. Though the powerful American army is still in Iraq to maintain law and order on the directions of Iraqi Governing Council, the transfer of power on 27-06-2004 (3 days ahead of the scheduled date) shall have brought about dramatic changes in the perspective of the Arab world. Observers proclaim that the force of anti-American propaganda could be very much blunted, and at least temporarily the rate of terrorist bombings have come down drastically. Whether this lull in bombing is regular and permanent is a question liable to be mentioned. But it must be conceded that the Bush policy of an early hand over has eased the tension considerably and the enemies of the Coalition have lost a vital weapon to beat the alleged imperial motives of Anglo-American occupiers. Also true that Bush was in dire urgency to bring some good news to the American electorate who are weighing their electoral option in November 2004. Good luck for Iraq that the American President Election is their Saviour and Iraq comes back to their hands, liberated from Saddam. Iraqis have to decide whether liberation is the genuine side of Iraqi nationalism, modelled by fundamentalist guerrillas who believe only in bombing raids. The Anglo American promise that the future Iraq will inherit a democratic government based on adult franchise, and majority rule, can be guaranteed only by stationing a permanent contingent of Anglo-US forces on Iraqi soil, and until the situation stabilises the stay of US forces may be indefinite also. This was done in South Korea, Japan and Western Europe and in each place for thoroughly different reasons and in thoroughly different methods and circumstances. When Japan was liberated by the United States, democracy was imposed on her, replacing militarism. In South Korea, after division there was the presence of the highly armed chauvinistic North Korea on the borders, and the US troops alone could guarantee the continued existence of the non communist south. Cold War was raging in high degree temperature and a Soviet threat to Western Europe was coming real. America wanted to prevent the arrival of dictators like Hitler, Mussolini and Tojo and the presence of American Allied Force did a double-purpose in Europe. Instead of being a naked occupation force, it was later re-arranged into a Euro-American coalition called NATO, with regional bodies like SEATO and CENTO. Most of Europe including volatile and indifferent democracies like Greece, and Italy re-established as democracies. If we examine the merit of US policy, it is evident that it was the military presence of America in these places that contributed to the democratic systems sinking roots and growing in most of the European States. Italy and France had powerful communist parties, and in the event of American neglect, a communist take over was very much on the cards in these countries. Greece was actually rescued from red-take over by American intervention. True, America realised the communist threat to Eastern Europe only very late, and this threat came due to the very generous policy adopted by FD Roosevelt towards Soviet Union. From 1945 to 1989, for about 44 years Eastern Europe lived within the Iron Curtain. It was Truman Doctrine and Marshall Plan that saved Western Europe, but it was at Yalta where the fate of Eastern Europe was sealed. After Truman there came no concrete policy to guarantee the liberation of the unliberated and to guarantee the safety and security of the free. True, there came the Eisenhower Doctrine and the Dulles brinkmanship-but it was in these times that the notorious East German riots failed, being crushed under Soviet armour, and the Balkanisation of Indo-China came to culmination through the disastrous Indo-China war, the French rout and the troubles in South Vietnam. The Dulles brinkmanship did not have any serious check on red-offensives and expansion. After 1954, the French felt deceived by America. Kennedy made a strident entry in Vietnam, but after a long war, America again capitulated in 1975. The high priests of capitulation were

Ford and Kissinger. In the aftermath of the Vietnam debacle, even Western Europe stood threatened under the irresolute, weak, Carter presidency and a Soviet take over of Western Europe was unattempted by Brezhnev, may be not for military reasons, but only because of the appalling size of the outrage. It was the Reagan Presidency which came prepared to defend the free world once again. In the Reagan era the calamitous capitulations of America the world over came to an end, but we find a robust, active internationalist in the White House only in George W. Bush. But for the Iraq war, I do not know if United States would have been wealthier by saving the war expenses in those countries and Iraq, but Bush brought back the power of the United States as the world policeman and this job is expensive always.

Winston Churchill was defeated at the polls in 1945, very immediately after he won the unwinnable Second World War for his countrymen, and this poll defeat leaves a trail of sad logic on the patriotism and responsibility of voters. Inflaming patriotism ought to take war as a life-and-death struggle. Now Al Gore (the more majoritarian winner but not the President elect) complains that the Iraq War is an unnecessary enterprise, even though too much American blood could not be shed on the battle fields of Babylon. So an Al Gore, as President in office, would have ratified the continuance of the murderous regime of Saddam, and the terrorists the world over would have been riding on terror waves frightening the world. Bush said good by to democratic passivity and indifference that welcomed terrorism everywhere. Atrocity regimes of Saddam, along with North Korea and Iran going nuclear remains the roguish possibility of international law. And "The Axis of Evil" the beautiful Bushite expression would have been a world-threatening reality. It is not philosophic to say that part of the happenings are human and part providential. A Bush victory in 2000 was only accidental. An American victory in Afghanistan and Iraq is a victory for human rights, and this entirely belongs to George W. Bush.

But the 2004 Election terror has hit George W. Bush also. In order to please his voter, Bush is now compromising his foreign policy agenda which mainly is the Iraqi programme. A look into the Bush policy will not suggest that he runs away from problems of crisis. It is common view that another President will only hesitate and even refuse to commit United States troops for an Iraqi liberation for fear that Iraq may turn out another Vietnam. But Bush want to end the isolationism of America and he wants to return to the days of FDR, when America intervened world wide. An Iraqi liberation is not a big military risk for the only earthly superpower - and never a risk comparable to America jumping into the First and Second World Wars. Now the problem is that most American Presidents do not lead, but only follow. Presidential power and policy are decided not by the adventurous and the patriotic but by stock-markets, street markets, media barons and journalists, if not by the gluttonous consumer. The media has become so indifferent to national questions as they call a military intervention an enterprise merely to kill American innocents. The media dissuades America from dangerous acts, and fear-complex becomes the hallmark of human gallantry. People are free, but democracies are not free, and much less free are her rulers. They recoil under any threat from anywhere. An activist ruler in America is checked and unbalanced by the media. In the midst of these inescapable imponderables against warfare the ruler should be exceptionally extraordinary to pull forward with a war programme. George W. Bush is swimming against the tide declaring that this turbulent course is the path of a superpower, wedded to guard human freedom.

Bush complains that the media does not want America win the Iraqi war, and from the patriotic path they deviate. The media never admits that America is a superpower and they pooh-pooh, the idea that America is the world policeman. They laugh at the suggestion that when America sleeps, there will be sabotage of world democracies. If Israel did not bomb the Iraqi-nuclear reactors two decades ago, there would have already arisen a nuclear armed Iraq with dangerously roguish nuclear pretensions against all her non nuclear neighbours in the Middle East, including Kuwait and Saudi Arabia. The world shudders at the thought of the Axis of Evil members (Iraq, Iran and North Korea) acquiring nuclear bombs. Once they got it, they, as masters and agents of state—terror will be eager to distribute it to terrorists world wide. Bin Laden will smuggle a bomb to bomb New York-and America will be facing the consequences of congressional media isolationism. The media is not only unmakes-they are the enemies of American adventurism. Once the world is informed that a 10 kiloton bomb is in the hands of a rogue terrorist, a city like London or New York or Mumbai or Shanghai will tremble with sleepless nights until it explodes and kills. When such bombs are widely distributed, such possibility being real when Iraq, North Korea or Tehran are acquiring it. Fortunately now the Nuclear Club comprise responsible nuclear powers like US, UK, France, China, India, Pakistan and Russia-who have taken strong precautions against a bomb or bomb grade uranium or plutonium falling into the hands of terrorists. But in this context the role of Pakistan still remains strange as her scientists themselves have declared recently that she sold atomic secrets for a price, and possible that those secrets found their way to North Korea. Pakistan was for sometime selling nuclear technology to willing states, and one such country is North Korea. North Korea's present behaviour shows that she is ready for playing any dirty game with its dirty bomb, and she can bargain for any ransom. It is this situation that is to be prevented by a superpower like the United States. To restrain such countries is the responsibility not only of US, but other nuclear powers like China, Russia, Britain and France also. Considering the human responsibility to protect life on earth, the other nuclear powers except US are not taking any active step to contain nuclear proliferation and nuclear roguism, and they leave the entire policing job to America. These States consider some bombs as friendly bombs and some others as enemy bombs. Till now, the world looks safe because we have disciplined and responsible bombs only. The whole humanity wants to live and flourish on this endangered earth, from which life should not be snuffed out, and that is not only the desire of all humans but the self proclaimed desire of all living beings-right from amoeba to the elephant. Nuclear roguism could be controlled till now, but whether it is containable in future is a question of world-watch policies. America is the only nuclear power who declares an active interest in stopping the proliferation of nuclear weapons and to have a definite strategy to dissuade, threaten or intimidate the nuclear hopefuls like Iran, Iraq, North Korea etc from bomb making. The other big powers like France, Britain, Russia, China, and India do not take a live role in containing these nuclear hopefuls. These countries are not uninterested, but their interest is confined to brokering between the rogues and superpowers, and they are content with these mediatory role. However, this role is non-activist as well as ambivalent. North Korea is known as a Chinese protege and it, should be easy for China to compel North Korea to demystify itself by de-nuclearisation. But China does not appear to put pressure on her client in that way, and instead leaves all difficult questions to America, who is left with the monopoly-duty of universal non-nuclearisation and de-nuclearisation. Have the other world powers no duty to humanity in protecting them from nuclear holocaust? Has the other world powers no responsibility in safeguarding the existing freedom of man with a right to enlarge it? Nevertheless, what is the role played by France and Germany in preventing the Saddam terror? In addition, what is their role in guaranteeing the freedom of the free and the future freedom of the unfree? Germany, just before the Second Gulf War, went to polls and in order to ensure the electoral win of Chancellor Schroeder and his party, made a sudden shift from the traditional NATO policy of solidarity with the United States. When US is taking the extraordinary step of ousting Saddam Hussein by arms, it is usual that NATO will follow her as it is the policy in the post-War World. If the European NATO members suddenly decide to dissociate with American policy, that is the making of a big dissent. Why France took the lead in disapproving of the American policy is difficult to assess, but it can be due to the attempted revival of Gaullism which sowed the seeds of discord in NATO in the sixties. De Gaulle, in his second coming in 1958, made an abrupt break with his country's policy towards America, and attempted a rapprochement with Soviet Union and made a powerful dissent in Nato. The reasons for this discord can be confusingly too many or too little. It can be the American neglect on French, Indo-China, where in the liberation war with Ho-Chi-Minh the French had to fight single-handed and lose in a very tragic capitulation, injuring the French pride. French were totally aggrieved of the callous stand taken by Eisenhower and his highly acclaimed brinkman Secretary of State–John Foster Dulles. The French believe that they had a very sad farewell from Indo-China, because of the unhelpful and indifferent policy of America. The Indo-china debacle was followed by another Anglo–French humiliation in Suez Canal in 1956, when they were stopped by Dulles from punishing Gamal Abdul Nasser of Egypt, and not a very easy thing for the French to forget. Britain, in 1954 once again under Winston Churchill ruled out any British assistance to the besieged French garrison at Dien Bien Phu. He told the visiting US Vice-President Nixon that if the British will not fight to keep India for them, he did not think they will fight to keep Indo-China for the French. America was ready to fight a bitter war, but only up to the last French man. This was moment of truth for the French. When De Gaulle came back to power in 1958, his first priority was for decolonising the French colony–Algeria, the largest African state. He was quick to disown that land and ready to bring back four and half a million French settlers long living in that territory. He designed an independent foreign policy and went out for a separate French rapprochement with Soviet Union, short of deserting NATO. Anti USism was very much writ on the foreign policy of De Gaulle and later that of the Gaullists. President Chirac is a Gaullist, and when the Second Iraq war came, he took an assertive stand that France will not side with American unilateralism for attack. But Chirac fails to answer some basic issues. Does he approve of the continued existence of a Saddam rule, which converted Iraq into a prison camp and reduced its people into economic and human, slavery? Should not United State take retaliation on the killers of

September/11? Is terrorism a threat facing the United States only - or a universal menace demanding a total war by all nations of the world? But now the inevitable NATO-solidarity is put to the sensations of a popular vote! Chirac has been closely followed by Schroeder who declared that unlike the German solidarity with NATO, as demonstrated in the First Gulf War, now it is a different question, and Germany will not join the Second holy war against Saddam. This Franco-German stand off was shock to George W. Bush, as it smacks of the disintegration of Nato. But all this the result of the unexpected end of Cold War, and the vanishing Soviet threat. When the Soviet threat is no more existent, what is the utility of NATO? There can be no NATO unity for unity's sake, when it has no use at all. Who will waste their money and blood for the freedom of Iraqis who do not want any freedom for themselves? The French say that if Iraqis want liberation, let them liberate themselves and they do not agree with the American monopoly right to wage proxy-liberation wars. If Saddam Hussein produces nuclear bombs, and sells it to Al Qaeda and they bomb democracy's places, they think the sure the targets can be New York and Washington, and not Paris and Berlin–and then why should Franco-Germans bother about Al Qaeda? They fail again to say what will be the reaction of Parisians and Berliners, when a rogue nuclear state sends their bombs to these cities? Is there any guarantee that the terrorists will strike only in America and nowhere else? France and Germany took a decision which is terrorist-friendly and this is a decision which endangers the war on terrorism. Nuclear bomb is a reality, and the world is afraid of it. To every danger, people react with caution as well as hope, and they hope that the feared dangers, will never come real. But hope could not make things. Safety minded people will have to take steps, which are effective and real. The fear on thermo-nuclear danger is real and overwhelming, but now that nuclear arms are under the safe-keep of being garrisoned by the possessed, is the only relief to the fearing non nuclear club. Now these would be victims fear that thermo-nuclear devices are going to be freely sold to terrorists who will carry it as grenades and lob it on any metropolis. If Saddam had produced a nuclear bomb, there is no doubt they will sell this bomb to Al Qaeda to bomb New York and annihilate its eight million citizenry. There will be no need nor relevance for a retaliation as Al Qaeda has no fixed abode and its organisation is ever-mobile and scattering world wide, as well as going underground. Then, who can punish them? Against this threat, Bush is going to the battlefield and his opponents call him fake-liberator or liberation enthusiast. On every danger leaders cannot sit complacent contending that events will take care of itself. More than the nuclear-possessed states, it is the nuclear unpossessed and the nuclear hopefuls who pose the gravest threat to humanity. Nuclear threat is not limited to humans only, and it threatens all forms of life. George W. Bush understands it, Rumsfeld and Cheney understands it; but Clinton and Kerry do not understand it. Kerry has only rhetorical remedies against terrorism, and nuclear terrorism. Kerry being soft on terror, has no action plan to stop the terrorists. When Bush stops terror, Kerry will not do that mean job. Kerry soft pedalling on the Franco-German desertion is really an anti-American act, as there is no justification for the terrorist friendliness of any NATO member.

Critical media and political adversaries violently attack Bush on his liberation war, rather his adventures in Iraq. They say it is not the business of America to free Iraq from the murderous rule of Saddam and this is denial of self-government to Iraqis. But they fail to explain the realities? What these people will do one day when Saddam will re-emerge with an atom bomb in his hands? If the Iraqi reactor had not been blown up in Israeli raids long ago. Saddam, very long ago, would have started nuclear blackmail in the Middle East, and the possibility of some nuclear unpossessed like Iran or Kuwait or Syria giving in to such blackmail also cannot be ruled out. Dick Cheney the US Vice- President says 'the possibility of Iraq acquiring a nuclear bomb in future and brandishing it in the roguish way justifies an attack on Iraq'. In the beginning stages Cheney the ultra rightist and the most feared war monger was not in favour of going to war in Iraq for a second time. But his reasons in favour of war got reinforced on wider premises, and the argument in Saddam acquiring a nuclear bomb rendering entire Middle East eternally sleepless is getting reinforced. The background of his history of mass-murders and genocides using poison gas or killer machines will only strengthen this argument. Saddam earned his reputation as a criminal against humanity several times. Now the media argues that a state bleeding with genocides, mass murders and butcheries is not guilty enough to be attacked. When judging the enemy, we look at the basic threats, he holds out against others, and to humanity in general. The crimes deserving revolution or overthrow are already committed by him a hundred times. But the indifferent allies ask what is the evidence that Saddam was in possession of WMD which can be launched against Anglo-US forces within forty five minutes of his decision to strike. That Saddam was capable of making and using it to kill innocent people and enemies at will, has been well demonstrated and documented before the world audience, but the same world is misinformed to ask if such weapons are recently re-discovered by the UN weapons inspectors. In fact it is a policy error of Anglo - American Coalition to have claimed that there is evidence of the existence of WMD stock-piles in Iraq, and such stocks can be murderously deployed within minutes. The existence of WMD shall never be the sole motive of the Coalition for invasion, but it was a wrong reason claimed as immediate provocation for action. For a moment we will forget WMD. Is not Saddam without ready-made WMD stockpiles, undeserving of attack and overthrow? The main motive of George W. Bush is that Iraq is a state which if allowed to perpetuate Saddam rule and his dynastic rule, with full freedom without sanctions, like North Korea, she will end up rogue state possessing nuclear weapons and threatening and intimidating the entire Middle East and the entire world. Saddam is a conqueror, and when the First Gulf War ended he saved his throne only under the wrongful generosity of Sr. Bush, and his rule-of-law general Collin Powell. The butcher of Baghdad re-emerged with multiple ferocity, and slaughtered all who came in the open seeking freedom of expression. The world knows he ended political dissent by systematic mass murders, and he slaughtered the entire political power establishment through mass-shootings in a night operation just after capture of power. Purges followed purges, and these were mass murders filling mass graves throughout the length and breadth of Iraq. Always he was crying for the blood of his enemies and he got it in large quantities. But surprising that the media argues the case of traitors, and political thugs and where do the morality of world politics take us? The U.S. Congress will not admit they have any intention to help Saddam. The media will not admit that they stand for the Saddam tyranny to perpetuate and flourish. But what they actually do is to disable and discredit the anti-Saddam movement, and in this way they want to destabilise and dismantle any infrastructure already laid by the coalition for democratisation of Iraq. It is in these circumstances that the Iraq lookers are forced to doubt the aim of the media in bringing democratic rule to that country.

Who are the forces who make all this violence and killings of hundreds every week? A single person can explode an RDX bomb in a crowd of a hundred thousand people and kill several hundreds, and this may look like a revolution in progress, just after the explosion. These terrorists can never be a majority as criminals in a society had never been. They are always a tiny-minority and this tiny minority, with the help of dangerous weapons can make their voice heard worldwide, through the explosive thunder of RDX, and the media comes forward to proclaim that there is going on a great revolution. If the Iraqi terrorists constitute a majority, they can comfortably take part in the coming elections and capture power. But they are not in a majority, and not forming even a fraction of it, and so they cannot stand to gain power through people's choice. When there is no chance to get a majority vote, the easy option before them is to sabotage the fast-emerging democratic process. Human Rights is the essential merit of democracy, and Human Rights can be guaranteed only by a democracy based on adult suffrage. World opinion can never raise the objection that Iraq shall not march into democracy. But the anti-democratic forces in Iraq do not want democracy, as they fear democracy and so they want to sabotage any attempt to sow its seeds there.

22
Those Fearing The Coming of Democracy In The Middle East

Terrorists are a small minority–and they exist only through very wealthy and powerful sponsors who stay underground. Terrorism is a political smuggling operation. If Iraq is threatened by an impending American colonisation, the majority of Iraqis will be opposing it and that must be an anti-majoritarian and anti-democratic programme. If there is terrorist bombings against colonisation, those bombs actually represent the free-will of the majority. But now, the question is for whom the bombs explode in Iraq. The Iraqi terror is no doubt caused by Saddam henchman and these bombs explode only after the war. The Anglo-American authorities are in a hurry to set up a democratic government in Iraq, and leave the country. The occupation history of the United States and in a good degree of United Kingdom speak that they leave occupied territory in a responsible way. Transfer of power to Indians was a huge task in 1947, and Indian leaders were prepared to wait for one or two years more for the actual transfer, once the grant of full independence at the earliest has been agreed to by Britain. New India wanted an orderly transfer. Unless transferred to a government in clear control, what follows in a new democracy is civil war, as we witness in many countries in Africa and Asia. America occupied many countries on different occasions, especially at the end of World Wars First and the Second. The transfer of power in Japan and Germany stands as monuments to their promise to vacate occupation, and hand over power to people. Japan and Germany today have one of the most well organised democracies in the world. America has power as well as wealth, and in keeping these promises sturdy, durable and dependable no doubt, American wealth has played a crucial role, as in the case of reconstruction of Europe and Japan after World War II. In that backdrop one will be forced to ask why the struggling-Iraqis cannot take advantage of these American promises and guarantees of good conduct, and march ahead as the power-house of democracy in the Mid-East. There is so much black gold under the soil of that country that Iraq can lead the Mid-East in democracy and economic progress. But saner thoughts on human values, human rights and majoritarian compulsions do not go well into the terror philosophy of Iraq. The terrorists do not want democracy and human rights; they do not want law and order and they do not want to reconstruct for prosperity. They want disorder, bomb explosions and mass killings, and they want to rule the majority by the terror of the minority. They fear prosperity and political stability as basic threats to their empire of disorder, and when Bush and Blair flaunt great promises to the blessed land of Euphrates and Tigris, the terror-captains reject it and ask for a country that flares up in bomb explosions. This minority is engaged in the rashness of a life and death struggle to stop the people of Iraq from tasting freedom and a liberal economy. This is the new imperialism of terrorist's. The media labours to invent visions of revolution in the voracious blood thirst of terrorist imperialism. George W. Bush pleads for an Iraq where man and his rights are free. Even if Bush is re-elected on his Iraqi platform, Iraq will not go for Iraqis but will go to the terrorists Iraq for terrorist only, and not for democrats!

Evidently Bush came to Afghanistan to take revenge on the September/11 culprits, and revenge has been taken by driving away Al Quaeda and Taliban to the White Mountains. Iraq has been punished, and if boiling revenge is the root cause of these punitive measures, then Bush by conquering the two terrorist states, shall be satisfied that he has completed the job very quick and well. Clauswitz says that war is merely an extension of political activity. In Korea, Gen. Ridgeway said negotiations are an extention of the battlefield; and now George W. Bush will say that democratisation and reconstruction are part of the invasion for liberation. Bush-Blair leadership after conquest has taken up the cause of democracy in Iraq a very daunting task for occupiers to do in the anti-democratic environment. The people of the Middle East have no acquaintance or interaction with democracy, and every democratic experiment has been immediately shadowed by dictators and religious fundamentalists. Algeria got independence in 1962, but immediately it fell into the despotism of Ben Bella, and then to army rule and there were only occasional honeymoons with democracy thereafter. The only country in the Mid-East being a full democracy is Israel, and that country is having only a struggling existence in the midst of monarchs, dictators and tyrants. And Israel being a democracy only intensifies the Arab hatred for democracy. To keep the dictators in the Muslim world care-free, the rulers draw support from the inimical existence of Israel. Egypt, Syria, Algeria and Iran are far away from democracy and they see any democratisation process as an unfriendly act. But as it is the rule of the people for the people, no country in the Middle East will openly oppose the coming of democracy in Iraq, but it is clear that any country in the region is not willing to tolerate the birth and growth of a new democracy in their midst. The old war horses like Egypt, and Iran also are in the suspect list. Saudi Arabia, Morocco, Syria, Algeria, Libya and the terrorists do not want democracy there to misinform and 'misguide' their people; and they view any inauguration of democracy in Iraq as a potential threat to the dictators in office. The only country they want in their midst is Israel, because she permanently guarantees the justification for the continuation of so many so called anti-Semitic dictators. Can George W. Bush hope that he is free to install democracy in Iraq in the way democracies are established in Japan and Germany? Even the pro-American Saudis will be praying for democracy to dig its grave in Iraq. So far as the Middle East is concerned, the founding of democracy in Iraq will be an unwelcome act. The present rebel attacks in Iraq is a deliberate attempt to sabotage the coming of a people's government. The rebels are capable of sending some suicide bombers who sacrifice their lives for the sake of money and very rich family supports. The attempt of the world media is to tell that terrorism augers a world revolution whereas it actually is a criminal act by a handful of people intent on defeating the reconstruction and democratisation of Iraq. A ruthless and decisive step by the Iraqi interim government and the coalition forces alone can defeat this process of sabotage, and establish a free government. Often in the decisive moment of victory the free world develops second thoughts on inflicting the fatal blow on the enemy and the victim at last escapes punishment. The message is that offenders can get away with their crimes, and this behaviour has done much harm to the cause of democracy as well a democratisation.

23
Afghan Invasion And The War On Terror

Crises opens the gates of great danger as well as greater opportunity. To lead a cliff-hanger political existence is the style of the brave and the courageous and Bush follows this course. Immediately on taking over office, Bush faced no serious national issue to struggle with. But then came the unexpected challenge after eight months. This is September/11 and he took it to heart as a national challenge facing America. Immediately after the attack, there prevailed total confusion, and Bush who was out of Washington was warned not to come to the capital for fear of the terrorists then on rampage. The confusion just after September/11 was a real test for America to see what she will do after a surprise nuclear attack. Now Bush is engaged in a war of survival in office, and instead of September/11, now comes November 2 2004, and the presidential fight is turning nasty. The Democratic contender Kerry says that Bush, when informed of September/11 in a private study delayed his response by seven minutes, and this is critical. True America is attacked but it is only a terrorist attack and not a nuclear attack, and the Bush delay may not be fatal. But will Kerry or anyone else keep up the promise, for revenge so completely and fulfil it by vanquishing two nations immediately? Against a surprise nuclear attack, America has the massive retaliation theory but here is only a civilian-plane crash on high towers. A shocked mind should sit back and respond, as knee jerk reactions by America will be too dangerous for world safety. Momentary response is needed only in a nuclear attack, but there also much caution and verification are essential. Response should be quick as well as reasonable. Some aides telling Bush that America is attacked does not mean that America is attacked with nuclear bombs. Literary exaggerations are to be understood rather than answered. But September/11 has given America a critical experience which she never had in the past. After the British attack in 1815, America never underwent a foreign attack on her soil, making a situation compelling her for swift retaliation, resistance and civil defence. There was the attack on Pearl Harbour in 1942, but the target, though an American territory was far away from the mainland and population centres, and therefore the people of America did not really feel they are actually attacked. Pearl Harbour was a naval war fought almost in the middle of Pacific, and in the fight America had only an initial reverse especially by substantial material loss. But the loss was immediately made up and America converted herself into war production. If the 1815 attack was a casual incursion, the first foreign attack on America can be September/11. All weapons of attack are domestic and the trigger-pullers alone are foreign.

The wars and battles America wages from the birth of the republic have been briefly referred to, but the great battles took place far away from American homeland and the domestic population never had the feeling that the enemy is at gate and they are in danger. In history, America never had the necessity to defend herself to protect herself. All wars were mainly fought for the immediate safety of others. This is the main reason leading Americans to complacency and isolation. Unless the home is really threatened who will think of the enemy? Though September/11 could be devalued as merely a terrorist attack, it was taken up as real attack, and America and Bush swore that this is invasion of America and the enemy will be punished. Usually Presidents and Prime Ministers make such declarations quite casually, but after sometime, people come ready to forget it as a dangerous enterprise, and the President too will be eager to forget it. But Bush did not and will not forget it. He wanted to take his revenge to the home of the unknown enemy, hiding however afar and intractable, who is Al Qaeda -reported well entrenched and head quartered in the Afghan mountains. Taliban was the ruler of Afghanistan and they harbour that wealthy and princely terrorist master brain-Bin Laden. Bush very much wanted Bin Laden-dead or alive as the main criminal in the September/11 crime. Bush asserts that western unity is possible only through strong American leadership. Bush never hesitates in the hour of crisis. He reminded America again and again that he will take revenge and his National Security Council went into conference continuously. The Council was asked to make a study for the invasion of Afghanistan which is the main centre of State sponsored terrorism. George Tenet–the now dismissed CIA chief, was complaining that though CIA had collected considerable details on terror and terrorists, and he made daily briefs to Presidents, no President including Clinton and Bush Jr. ever said anything definite or suggested any concrete programme of action in counter-terrorism. Bill Clinton was informed of the top terrorists, but he refused to sign an order directing the targeting and elimination of these terrorists by the CIA, and in that way the CIA lay there unadvised and ignored—Unlike the toppling game played against Mohammad Mossadeque in Iran in 1953 by CIA, no direct authorisation was received from the White House to target and murder terrorists. Funds were also not allowed to these projects, and the anti-terror war-front remained a theoretical non-entity. Red-tapism sat comfortably on counter-terrorism moves. George W. Bush will allow these requests, but only after September/11.

Bush declared before the Security Council that he wanted to attacks Afghanistan and the Taliban, and wanted to flush out and punish terrorists. In the NSC, there were hawks and doves. Dick Cheney, the Vice-President is a hawk; the Defence Secretary Donald Rumsfeld is a hawk. Collin Powell is a dove and Condoleezza Rice–a moderate but again the President is a hawk; and so the Afghan invasion on the majority decision of NSC, was a foregone conclusion. The programme needs new friends around Afghanistan but now continental Europe looks the other-way, and this was disturbing to the White House. The two big Europeans - Germany and France, who followed America and plunged into the First Gulf War with men, munitions and money will not come this time to Afghanistan. When they refuse America had to go it alone and battle. Poland, Spain, and Italy agrees to come; and Britain will support and some junior members of the European Union will also come. The NATO flank stands divided, for the first time in history, and so America must go in search of new friends. President Karimov of Uzbekistan, by dollaring, cajoling and promises, came forward to help by granting landing rights for troops and planes and this was big break-through. Putin was pacified by Bush, and the promised that in any case he will not come to oppose America. Putin was persuaded also to sell arms to the Northern Alliance–the enemy of Taliban–and ultimately CIA paid Russia for these arms. Secret military missions entered Afghanistan through air and mountain borders, CIA made an entry in the North with dollar bundles and the leaders of the Northern Alliance came one by one into their secret enclave in north Afghanistan. Those in urgent need of money, mainly to pay soldiers and weapons, were paid by CIA in dollar bundles. Tenet says the dollars paid by CIA to the Northern Alliance chiefs were less than 70 million, but the returns were huge. There were covert operations, and the outside world got only confusing signals regarding the progress made by the American advance team in Northern Afghanistan. On occasions, Bush was monitoring the operation which was making steady progress.One Afghan leader on whom the United States had placed high hopes was Fahim-but he was always postponing and postponing by one excuse or other. His changing demands were all fully met, but still he will not mobilise his forces for a fight. At last America decided to go ahead with the attack, and the main job was done by Northern Alliance. America supplied high-tech arms and equipment. As well there were the arms got from Russia and others. The city of Morad fell and it was big news in Washington. Rice and Bush were elated. The entire operation lasted only three weeks. When Marad fell, the total US army personnel inside Afghanistan were less than 400, and the main operation was carried out under their guidance by Northern Alliance. The large induction of US ground troops occurred only afterwards. The Taliban forces retreated into the White Mountains leaving large quantities of arms and equipment in caves and secret storages. These were captured by Northern Alliance and US troops. Bin Laden is reported hiding in Tora Bora in the White Mountains–or in the border mountains in Pakistan.

It was mainly for the mopping up operation and maintenance of law and order that American troops were deployed in large numbers. These troops are still there. The counter-attacks and terror attacks the coalition forces are now facing in Iraq did not occur in Afghanistan. The people in Afghanistan are more compliant and they seemed fed up with the continuing anarchy and civil war that subverted their economy and peaceful life for more than two decades. After the expulsion of Taliban from country side, the Coalition forces could establish quick bridge-heads in different parts of the country, and the relief operations could be widened and made practical and effective. The casualties on the American side and the Northern Alliance were small, and the casualties on the Taliban side though not known, cannot also be very large as the operation did not involve long and bitter battles. Bin Laden and his coterie the main executors of the Twin Towers at Ground Zero are not yet nabbed and they are hiding. Reports that Bin Laden is killed in bomb raids, are falsified by the reports in the Al Jozeera TV, and now almost confirmed that Bin Ladan is in full control of his worldwide terrorist network, targeting USA and Europe. Like ten thousand police men chasing an eluding thief, and missing him every time, the American attempt to nab Bin Laden continues an impossible task. Laden is very much active and terrorising. In the meanwhile America imposed an orange alert throughout its territory to prevent a new Bin Laden strike, especially against financial institutions like World Bank, and IMF in Washington. In Europe also red-alert has been clamped on vital centres and Bin Laden and Al Quaida continues to rule the bombs, terror and explosions. The terrorist now strike in capitals like Madrid and force governments to withdraw from Baghdad. They abduct foreigners and brainwash them to obey the voice of terror.

The Afghan operation was a comparatively, light job for America and they managed it to a satisfactory completion. Here the bitter experience that Russia had in the 1979-89 period did not confront the United States. The US and the US policy of choosing the Northern Alliance to administer the country appears to have gone well with Afghan people and revolters. Immediately after the war, America declared her intention not to occupy the country, but help it in self-determination, reconstruction, democratisation and restoration of law and order. The process is going on and the interim government of Karzai is attempting to manage the administration well especially in the cities and country side, but perhaps not in the mountain area where the Taliban hides. The Afghan King Sahir Shah–the long time exile of Rome-returned to his country but he is not allowed his second coronation. Karzai has promised elections, and there is strong opinion that elections shall be held under UN auspices, to gain credibility. But the Red Cross workers and the UN offices in Kabul were threatened by Taliban. Though these threats are not as powerful and devastating as in Baghdad, the terrorist threats are still there, but the quantity of blood shed in the aftermath of Afghan liberation is not as much. But in the face of threats and the bomb blasts the UN operations in Afghanistan stands suspended. Any how Afghan elections are going to be a reality.

In the war on terror, America could make significant progress in organising world opinion and in incorporating the assistance and participation of powerful countries in Middle East itself. Saudi Arabia, Jordan, Turkey, Egypt, Pakistan, and UAE are in the assistance group. Al Queda is very active in Kashmir and therefore Pakistan has difficulty in restraining and obstructing their terror, but under severe American pressure, Musharraf has agreed to impose restrictions and also to arrest the active operatives in the country. Many top militants are already held in Islamabad and many of them are deadly too. The world powers including Russia and China usually found at the opposite end of the US policy line, also come forward to oppose terrorists. Here too the Bush diplomacy has made important gains. Except France and Germany, Europe as a group are rallying behind the Anglo-American coalition in the war on terror. September/11 has been made into a big issue only because George W. Bush made it a war issue. The Madrid bombing or the Indonesian bombing too developed into world issues. In the Madrid bombing, many hundreds died and this is the biggest terror strike in Europe. For another American president September/11 would have been simply a terrorist attack which is merely an accident, and Al-Queda would have gone unchallenged and unpunished. It was the daring's of George W. Bush and his adventures that built up the huge anti-terror platform that focuses the terrorist bodies to world audience, to target and to destroy. The war is going on and the credit for this war on terror will go to George W. Bush only.

24
Farewell To Surrenders And The Resolve To Win

George W. Bush has been renominated Republican candidate for 2004 President Election, and that his team does not undergo a shake up, evidences his determination to follow the hawkish line on terrorism. Unlike many predecessors, he is having a mission in office and, not following a policy of meeting things adhoc. After September/11, the president of the United States could have remained aloof from trouble-some engagements, saying that it is simply a terror-attack, but only with larger casualties, and it does not deserve to be considered a terrorist revolution; and the whole event would have gone into history as a big crime deserving only police action. But Bush took it differently. It is now a regular feature of political dissent that a handful of people with bombs, will enter the scene as suicide-bombers, take large number of people as hostage, demand ransom, and then release or kill prisoners. A dramatic start with capture of innocent people as hostages and asking for satisfying the impossible demands of captors is a direct assault on human rights. Once asking ransom for releasing hostages was the robbers' job, but now that of the revolutionary. This terror culture of intolerance and bargain now assume new shapes. This international ganging up of criminals is to be stopped, but how this is to be done is the difficult question. When remedies reach a blind ally, the rulers ignore it to be met adhoc.

Terror attacks are an attempt to impose the will of the criminal against the will of the majority. A terrorist striking at government or military establishments can be lauded and lionised for his courage and adventure, but not for his ideology. A terrorist who selects innocent people as targets, for destruction and revenge, is doing no political service. He acts only as criminal; and that criminality assumes a new depravity when it wants to drink the blood of innocents, and the more depraved it becomes when they ask for money for sparing lives. This is not revolution, but banditry.

Why Jr. Bush declared war on terror and he moves and shakes the tremendous military arsenal of America to frighten those handful of criminals, many do ask. Are terrorists a worthy opponent of a superpower to be fought and vanquished, and whether the silliness of the terrorist threat has been blown out of proportion only to manufacture a cause for conducting wars anywhere in the world? I have argued that any conqueror, to fool his audience, wants to present a face-saving moral formula, that he has been persuaded to go to war on irresistible moral pressures. But the real cause is his certainty and confidence that his arms are capable of conquest, annexation and victory. The question whether war on terror is a worthy business for a superpower to undertake is a political question mainly intended to annoy. Terrorists are an international fighting force, but having no common ideology except terror, and each gang fighting for different causes. They fight on separate motives but adopt the common medium of terror. As I am writing these lines, hundreds of Russian schoolchildren and parents at Beslan in Northern Ossetia in Russia are taken hostage by Chechen terrorists and they are attempted to be rescued by storm troopers. These terrorists want a big package, to be granted by Russian Government including the release of Chechen prisoners of war. But the Putin government is determined not to cave in for any terror demands, and the terrorists in Russia are continuously disappointed of this stand of Putin. The world has seen warriors fighting warriors, but not warriors avoiding warriors and directing their fight against innocents. When x is the murderer, why do they kill innocent y; and the world does not pick up that logic. This is again the Vietminh strategy of frightening away the population from aiding or joining or conspiring with government forces. True, the large majority of innocents is the guilty target!

The terrorists can organise into a world body and incorporate themselves into an international army, but before that dangerous consolidation, Bush wanted to strike back. Here I describe the Bush response to September/11 as articulate preventive and effective in taking on terrorism the world over and with diplomatic effects being more dramatic. Without this massive Bush response, September/11 and would have died down into a usual human tragedy, liable to be forgotten in due course; and by the time the Twin Towers and its thousands of martyrs would have gone behind human memory. But the Bush strategy keeps those slain alive. There are train accidents, bus accidents and plane crashes and shipwrecks in which thousands die, but only to be forgotten after bursts of emotion and mournings. Now only because of the Bush strategy of a declared war on terror, it has become increasingly difficult for terrorists to operate world-wide and take not the guilty, but the innocents world over, for ransom. True, terrorists make violent strikes, but do they succeed? When Bush was taking September /11 as a challenge, that lead was accepted and followed by the world, and a new motive and morality have been introduced into the philosophy of war on terror. In fact, the great majority of the United Nations has felt the need to speed up and re-organise their anti-terror machines, only because of the leadership George W. Bush is giving. Because of this leadership, today the war on terror is a scheme at the top of agenda of world leaders and their determination to fight terror has been reinforced.

Whatever its defaults and shortcomings, democracy is very much the form of government more acceptable to people, and this peoples' power is based on majority opinions. To make a public assessment of how much of peoples' opinion has been restricted, trampled upon and overrun by the demands of terror in the world, is now overdue. The Chechen fighters know that Putin fought the terrorists in the Moscow theatre crisis, and their demands went into pieces. Now the school hostage crisis at Beslan also ended in the mass-murder of schoolchildren and innocents and the terror demands are all rejected, all terror sacrifices-going waste. Because of the bungling and inefficacy of the storm troopers, the death toll is one of the highest after September/11, and unofficial estimates put it at more than 440 and Putin himself is aggrieved of the murderous bungling of the rescue mission. He admits failure in the counter-terrorism machinery. Even if the Russian government kept silent, the toll would not have been higher, some will argue. But in Iraq, hostage takings have some rare success stories also to tell. The Spanish government following an election promise to the people, have withdrawn their token contingent from Iraq, and though this climb-down is not in response to any terrorist threat, this is a terrorist-friendly act. When some Indonesian workers were taken hostage in Iraq, the government immediately capitulated and withdrew its small military contingent from Iraq. This is another success story, welcoming terrorists to more audacious moves. But the Chechen guerrilla offensive failed in the face of resolute defiance by President Putin. Only due to bungling by the rescue teams, the rescue-operation could produce only mass victims, but terrorists achieved nothing except the wrath of Russians.

The incidence of plane-hijackings came down drastically with the clamping of strict security restrictions on air travel, especially in the Americas. Now terrorists employ driverless-cars with car bombs. To attack they park bomb-loaded cars in crowded places and the driver flees. The car bombs, which are time-bombs, explode after an interval and kills innocents. These changes in operation techniques show that terrorists themselves have become safety conscious, and they want to keep as many terrorists alive as possible. Why they target innocent civilians ? The terrorist frightens the innocents and avoid a direct fight with government forces. When ordinary civilians are taken hostage, kinsmen and patrons make an immoral, cowardly plea to the government to surrender to terror demands, and this reaction is only natural; but this peoples' attitude projecting their personal sorrow in front of state interests, will be doing great harm to anti-terror programmes. On the other hand, if a band of terrorists are fighting with soldiers, and if these soldiers are taken hostage, there will be no call by the relatives of the soldiers that the war has to be stopped to save the life of soldiers. If such plea is made, then thousands of parents of thousands army men will take to the streets demanding governments to surrender to the enemy, only to save the life of their soldier sons, and what a ridiculous plea? When the enemy attacks, there is no plea for a surrender even in the face of greatest danger to life. But when the same enemy attacks under the mask of a terrorist, the people assail the government for their failure to appease the enemy and save the hostages and this is new logic. Why the world failed to accept that terrorism is war until Bush declared it a war?

When the Twin Towers were attacked on September/11 2001, there was no warning and no revolting demands made with conditions to satisfy them. Long before September/11, Bin Laden and Al Queda have established and widened a world net-work of terrorists to strike at important targets. The motive ought to be to punish the United States. But remember that on September/11, 2001, America had no plans to invade Afghanistan and Iraq. When Afghanistan was invaded by Russia in 1979, America was on the side of Taliban. In the Gulf War, 1991 the terrorists were not targetted, and the main aim was to liberate Kuwait. What was the immediate provocation for Al Queda to attack on September/11, the world will never know, as war on terror was not in the top agenda of US before September/11. Terrorists made no warnings and they made no demands but they targeted, only to destroy, and this is a new phase in terrorism. September/11 was simply punishment and no bargain. They took no hostages, and perhaps they wanted to take the entire United States hostage. The terrorists might have hoped that even after the September/11 massacre, the terrorism business, as usual, can go on unharmed after the first reactions of shock and horror, are over. But everything in consequence depends on the person of the offended ruler, and for terrorists, George W. Bush alone gave a new lesson, Bush declared that September/11 is invasion of America, and he is declaring war on terror. Such declarations always come, but in real practice there will be nothing more than declarations and protests, and the guilty go free. But regarding Bush's September/11, the terrorist calculus has gone wrong.

It is the political moral that a terrorist comes to attack only to punish the enemy and commit the extreme sacrifice, and never to return, home. For a suicide bomber, the future punishments are no deterrence. Then how to prevent the terrorist and what are the preventive steps. Terrorists shall have an abode, where he is harboured, trained and motivated. To crush the terrorist, the harbouring states are to be punished. There are sponsoring states, but who are these states? Afghanistan was a sponsoring state, and Bush will invade and destroy the terror facilities there. He went to Afghanistan, drove out the Taliban and the world's most deadly terror-strongholds and camps were destroyed. He did not stop there. He occupied that country, installed a new government there under Karzai, and now planning to establish a democratic regime, and popular elections are round the corner. The terrorists in Afghanistan are on the run including their chief Bin Laden, and the rest is recent history to be retold. Perhaps the first democracy in the Middle East can be Afghanistan, and its founder George W. Bush.

Bush did not stop in Kabul. He was bidding his time for the Baghdad putsch and the overthrow of Saddam. Iraq surrendered and Saddam was overthrown. After some months Saddam was captured a broken soul from an underground hide-out near Tikrit. Why this modern Hitler did not choose the heroic path of suicide, and preferred to be the prisoner of the enemy? If he fought and died in the battle front, what would have been his place in the fable of Arab heroes! But he chose the humiliating, demeaning path of surrender and this surrender only adds to the credit of Bush presidency.

Now that the Bush-Cheney team of Republican hawks have been renominated for the November election. The American voter is presented with very difficult options. In 2000 Bush won not because of majority but because of luck. But in 2004, he has to win because of merits of governance and then the people of America ask so many questions? To answer Bush must be a good debater too.

Has George W. Bush endangered United States by rushing to the Afghan-Iraq War? In the post-war period, the Afghan -Iraq wars are the only complete victory America can claim. In all other wars Korea, Vietnam, and the first Gulf War, there were only failures, humiliations and half-victories. To post-war America, Bush now brings a full victory and because of Bush, America is again the policeman of the world. Bush has leadered a world revolution by electrifying the world conscience on the urgent need to fight terrorism before it swallows up the rights of man. Bush has a programme for the almost impossible democratisation of Iraq and Afghanistan, and this is possible only if he continues in office for some more years. If Afghanistan and Iraq also choose democracy as the basis for their future government, the territory of world democracy will again be expanding and the territory of terror shrinking.

The prophets of doom foretelling an American economic collapse due to Bush's mismanagement, now look wrong because of a fast recovery and creation of hundreds of thousands of new jobs. Clinton was lucky to enjoy the results of the good works done by his predecessors, and he was riding a prosperity wave. He was enjoying the blessings of a dynamic economy. But the Bush achievements are more momentous than economic. America, while going for a new war, will be looking back to all the wars she waged, and the battles she won and lost. If she looks at Vietnam, she will be shocked of the magnitude of the tragedy and the loss of face, as if never again she will venture into fighting. But if she looks at the two world wars, the story is of complete triumphs. She led the world forces and led them to historic victories that dismantled empires and begot new democracies, and unfortunately failed to prevent many dictatorships. Many post-war democracies derived their life support from the money and arms of America, and even now, this American service goes on. If Bush can convert Afghanistan and Iraq into new democracies, that will be a new revolution in the Middle East. The examples of Japan and Germany–the post-war American colonies will delightfully smile at his proposal. Has America become endangered or safer by making Germany, Western Europe, France, Japan, Italy, and Greece democratic? When isolationist fellow travellers like France and Germany hesitate to take part in the Bush march, should America too shrink back from her global responsibilities? Security is the consequence of courage, and not the consequence of fear. Kerry, the Democratic opponent admonishes America that she has become unsafe because of Bush. In saying so, Kerry may be ignoring the meaning of words courage and cowardice, safety and unsafety. Do the American people know the difference? They will tell it only in November 04.

What is the political justification for an attack on Afghanistan and Iraq? Wars are decided not on the basis of its causes, but on its consequences. There is no use in enquiring what are the causes that cause a war. The war in Iraq and Afghanistan may cause a revolution in these countries, and as a first step, the people are placed in the path of liberation and freedom, but it is up to them to choose. Bush invaded these lands, defeated the opposing forces and his next attempt is to re-invent their political life in the democratic way. Having the massive superiority of arms and technology, it is no surprise America defeated these countries and occupy them. Any powerful country can inflict a military defeat on a less powerful one, and leave the place in utter disorder: and civil strife would be the result with none accountable and responsible. There is not a more unfortunate situation than civil war and anarchy. But what the rebels in the Middle East desire the most is civil war and disorder, and not peoples' government. America and Britain have expressed their intention not to continue in Iraq, once elections are held and a responsible government takes over. Bush pursues this policy, and he is facing the challenges of terrorists against completion of this job. If an orderly government elected by people are placed in power and a vigorous economic policy is pursued, Iraq can be transformed into a powerful state in the very near future. They possess so much of resources, especially oil. But once democracy is established, the leader coming to power must be disciplined and principled enough to hold elections and hand over power to the next elected government. It is at this juncture that difficulties arise because of absence of precedents and democratic tradition. Once reaching power, no Middle-East ruler voluntarily vacates office and his new dictatorship will be his pleasure. Can Anglo-American authorities prevent this accident, coming to these people, once democracy is established in Afghanistan and Iraq? The occupation powers can maintain a force in these countries to see the democratic process stabilise, and also see there are periodic elections and orderly change of rulers. To ultra revolutionaries this may be a very objectionable idea, but the post-war history of countries like Japan, Germany, South Korea etc. will support this conclusion. There were stationed occupation forces in Japan and Germany after the conclusion of war, but after transfer of power, the stay of smaller contingents of occupation forces in Japan, Germany and South Korea has indirectly contributed to democracy's stabilisation process. Till 1951, in Japan and till 1949 in Germany, there were occupation forces and these forces had decisive roles in these places. The occupiers, being democrats, like USA and UK, their presence also helped the evolution of democratic process, in these countries. The emergence of a new dictator or tyrant in these countries-which claim long histories of dictatorships, tyrannies and military governments shall have been prevented by the occupation forces in the beginning. Even the presence of NATO forces in Europe shall have contributed to the stability of democracy in these lands, as no venturing dictator will emerge before the eyes of these powerful military forces. While NATO prevented the emergence of un-democratic forces, the Warsaw Pact saw that no democratic force emerges in Eastern Europe. In Turkey and Greece, military dictators have emerged in spite of the standing NATO units, and so this cannot be an invariable rule in all places. But in the formative years of post war democracy in Japan and Germany, the presence of occupation forces have exercised its decisive influence in the growth of the democratic system. The hoped for practical side of democracy in Iraq and Afghanistan can be more primitive, rudimentary and experimental, being infant experiences in a completely anti-democratic environment. The presence of an Anglo-American standing army for some time more will be a right step for the sake of democracy in these places. Aristotle said 'sometimes force is to be used to keep man free'.

The Bush war on terror, because of the massive diplomatic offensive he launched and the decisive military strikes he made has attracted the world's attention as a big policy issue. But the world media is yet to formulate a clear policy of its own on counter-terrorism, and they never gave unequivocal support to American war on terror. Terrorists have no permanent abode, they having only a fugitive existence. They cannot have a permanent abode also as their clandestine existence is their main strength. Once countries like Libya, Sudan, Iran, Syria, Afghanistan, etc. were terrorist harbouring states, but now they disown them, and this is the result of a strongly coordinated American policy under Bush. As in the case of the First World War, which was waged nearly a century ago, the causes of war are yet to be probed and discovered by specialist researchers, but the real cause of the Second Gulf War is George W. Bush. The fall out of the Bush war on terror has created a world platform against the terror machine growing every day more menacing. It was the Bush adventures on terror, that took the war to the two sponsoring states, Afghanistan and Iraq, and in the case of Afghanistan it was really a war against the world-trotting terrorist out-fit, Al Qaeda. On the Iraqi question, it became evident that Saddam was not harbouring a better terrorist than he himself, and so his murderous regime toppled. It is in Iraq that America is facing conflicts and complexities against political transition into democracy. This transition will be definite, certain and smooth only if George W. Bush is re-elected. John Kerry may do it or may not do it in Iraq. On the other hand, if Kerry makes an open declaration that he is firm on his support for Iraqi democratisation, a political continuity can be assured. But Kerry stands for criticism and criticism is the hallmark of a policy vacuum. Eisenhower was critical of Truman's Korea policy, but as president, he could only capitulate in Korea. Bush is for strengthening the forces of democracy and for suppressing the forces of terror, and he is unrelenting on this principle. But there appears breaches in the fortress of democracy, and now we hear the dissenting voices of Germany and France on the manner the terror war is progressing, and this European dissent is a big question in the NATO phalanx. But the dissenting NATO members are actually weakening the war on terror.

Bush went to the war of rampage after September/11, and he is definite about his aim to hit at terrorism. Only 105 days after September/11, Afghanistan has been captured. On the basis of electoral vicissitudes, he refuses to change his policy on terror, and the only issue he came ready to compromise is the handover of power to Iraqis on 27-06-2004, and as a first step the appointment of an Interim Governing Council under Allawi. America and Britain are ready to pull out, once a democratically elected government has taken charge. This declaration must satisfy the common man, and therefore in the normal course, the prospect of the ultimate power coming to the hands of the people should satisfy the feelings of the majority. And the remaining problem is the terrorist, and the revolting ultranationalists, possibly loyal to Saddam or Al Queda or any other political or regional outfit.

Will America vote for George W. Bush for whose overthrow by election defeat, the enemies of America and their allies are hoping and praying for? Will the people of America vote out Bush and a moderate will come to the White House? If George W. Bush is defeated, the terrorists can win without battles. Who can say that Kerry will live up to the wishes of terrorists, who hope to come in the open and once again let loose the reign of terror? Senator Edward Kennedy and Al Gore (the real President-elect 2000) have criticised Bush for invading

Iraq and Afghanistan just for the sake of flushing out terrorists. From this soft-response, the world knows what Al Gore as President, would have done in response to September/11. Al Gore would not go for an Afghan or Iraqi invasion, and the most he would order is to conduct a national mourning and some police action, and world terrorism will again be on the upbeat, and Al Queda will continue to threaten the peace of the world. If instead of FDR, it was another isolationist in the White House in 1941, America would have refused to enter the Second World War, as she faced no direct threat to her territories. Allies would be losing the war, the Axis could dominate the world, and Asia would have gone under Japanese occupation, and Europe and Russia under Hitler who would build the 1000-year Reich. There would have been no free India and no Communist China. Only because of American entry into war, all these Axis dreams went in smoke. It is on these reasons that Hitler ran into ecstatic tantrums when he heard the news of Roosevelt's sudden death in 1945, March. The terrorists may hope for the electoral victory of John Kerry, and this is a clearly possible alternative when compared to the wishes of Hitler and Tojo. Will America in November 2004, throw away George W. Bush, and compromise on war on terror? In spite of being a terrorist favourite, whether a vote for Kerry will be a vote against terror, the people are in serious doubt only because of the Kerry evasions and vacillations. The interests of America cannot be vacillating.

Before the Iraq-Afghan war, America suffered under terrorists. The embassy bombings at Kenya and Tanzania which left hundreds dead, the terrorist attacks on Americans in Lebanon and Germany, the notorious and long hostage taking in Tehran in 1979-80, when 53 American hostages were held, teased, insulted and humiliated; the plane-hijackings and the Lockerbie bombing of PAN AM by Libyan terrorists, the attacks on other American embassies world-wide and ultimately the September /11, 2001 attack on World Trade Centre are the terrorist strikes that challenged the power of the Unite States. But these major terrorist attacks took place before the American intervention in Afghanistan and Iraq, and not after. Terrorists must have deep grievances against the superpower, but the unending cause is Palestine. There may be changing causes, but for any enterprising world criminal, America is a permanent obstacle. And more than anything else, challenging the power of America is in the highest revolutionary fashion and example.

After September/11, the air travel restrictions clamped over have reduced the incidence of plane hijackings in the United States. After this attack at Ground Zero, stringent restrictions were imposed and the terror attacks in the United States came down almost to zero. Still the intelligence agencies CIA and the FBI inform that attacks are being planned by Al Qaeda and others, and more terrible strikes are in the offing. September/ 11 followed by massive bomb attacks in Indonesia that claimed more than 300 deaths. A very important case is the hostage taking in Russia. Two years ago it led to a great tragedy in a Moscow. Theatre where a terror camp was stormed by troops, but the death tolls still rising high. When these lines are written, there is another crisis in Russia shaking the world conscience. At Belsan in Northern Ossitia, hundreds of school children and parents are taken hostage by Chechan rebels and it appears that the Putin government as their established policy, have rejected their demands. But the rescue operation proved the most tragic and costliest after September/ 11. Official figures put casualties at 320 dead but unofficially placed at more than 440. The rescue operation was bungled wholly, when even without government intervention the death toll would not have been higher. The counter terrorism machinery in Russia still remain inefficient. But the terrorist must be disappointed that all their demands failed and the sacrifices produced no results. Terrorists may either become frustrated; or they will come again with added malice. But failures, what ever its revolutionary fervour and reach, will only discourage and dampen the spirit of the terrorist and his sponsors. India won the war against Sikh terrorists, only by fighting them and not by compromise. Even 3 years after September/11, if there is no major attack in the United States and Britain—the open challengers of world terrorism at present—what conclusion do we reach? Terrorists may be wealthier, better organised, inveterate, articulate and adventurous, but their operational and punishing efficiency are seen reduced. The main reason is that sponsoring states like Libya, Sudan, Syria, Iran, Afghanistan etc, are forced to have rethink on their support, because of measures of massive retaliation and war. The open war declared by America and Britain, and the invasion and occupation of the sponsoring states of Afghanistan and Iraq has made a new impact. Libya comes forward to establish new ties with the West guaranteeing civil behaviour in future. North Korea-another rogue state--capable of nuclear-terror also is, in the American hit list, but now both sides attempting compromises to prevent escalations. Iran is another suspect, but she must be happy that her deadly foe-Saddam is in captivity. But the Iranian nuclear programme appears to be more ambitious than peaceful and her conduct evidences a decent attempt to become a nuclear power in the near future. America views this attempt with concern and warnings are issued many times. Iran fears even an Israeli strike against her nuclear installations. But now Iran is not projecting herself an enthusiastic terror-sponsor. And in the face of the Bush offensives, Sudan and Syria are not likely to play major roles in terror-sponsorship. Because of George W. Bush and his adventures on terror, the offensive power of terrorism is on the decline, and this reality the world is coming to accept. But the world cannot measure the correct strength and weakness of terrorists, as they live and organise in the under-world. For these devastating anti-terror drives including war Bush committed his political future wholly including his re-election chances. The continuing of this anti-terror war is essential for the safety not only of the United States but the entire world. Terrorism & Co. incorporated is a major threat as it manifests itself violently through the bosom of the earth, and Bush alone has shown the audacity to take the terrorism-bull by its horns. Whether this anti-terror policy is to continue, the answer lies with the American people.

A statesman is never judged on his textbook brilliance and moral preachings. As president, the Bush career is attacked on reasons irrelevant to a statesman. Churchill was a dull student in school, but he was a great warrior. True, even into his forties Bush was a failure. He failed in all programmes his father made repeated success. I repeat what a British Labour Party member said of the Bush team, 'their hawkish militancy is, exceeded only by their diplomatic and political illiteracy'. Others believe that Bush is merely a stupid fellow wrongly chosen by the Republican Party, but rightly rejected by the electoral majority, but again wrongly chosen by the American Supreme Court for an, unfit White House job and so he will do only stupid, dangerous things. And more damaging comments are in the making by enemies. When he failed in all places his father succeeded, he succeeded in the only job his father failed and that is as President of the United States. He alerts all statesman of the world of America's responsibilities towards planet earth, and towards the free-world in particular. He is conscious of the need to maintain and monitor the non-violation of rights of man and its perpetuation. But more than anything else, he is conscious of the dangers staring at and threatening human rights, and the American capability and promise to protect it. He is conscious of the power of America to guarantee freedom, and he knows how to employ that power to the advantage of humanity in general. Instead of sleeping over the sins of terrorism with a sick conscience, he went out to punish the criminal in adventurous engagements. He will not allow the military might of America to languish and rust in the face of injustice but he employs it to defend the United States and the United Nations. Even if powerful allies desert midway, he is undaunted, because still the American superpower can handle a crisis single handed though with greater exertion. His enemies focus on his petty faults but suppress his spectacular gains in war and peace, and they are not playing the political level field. He is not a scholar when scholars themselves do not make statesmen. Aristotle was the greatest scholar of his times, but his unscholarly disciple-Alexander is the greatest conqueror in history. Here is George W. Bush, a very ordinary brain making an extraordinary statesman.Will America too say so in November 2004?

Bibliography

In a book of this nature, references can be limited as well as extensive. The nature of this book is biographical, political, constitutional, diplomatic and legal and the references to law are more an extension of a book of narration. The author himself is lawyer. The books mentioned below, supplied me many kinds of materials-may be an assortment of information. The hundreds of essays and politcal articles made use of are impossibly large to be cited and referred to here. Some books for which written notes are available alone are mentioned here, especially those read quite recently.

1. *Media and Soveignty,* Munroe E. Price.
2. *Grammer of Politics,* Harold J. Laski.
3. *Indian Government and Politics,* Hans Raj.
4. *Congress Confronts the Court,* Colton C. Campbell.
5. *The Right Man,* David Frum.
6. *Bush At War,* Bob Woodward.
7. *Law's Empire,* Ronald Dworkin.
8. *Basic Law of Germany,* Press and information office Government of the Republic of Germany.
9. *Constitutions in Demorcratic Politics,* Vernon Bagdanor.
10. *Collapse of the Third Republic,* William A. Shirer.
11. *Marx on Globalisation,* David Renton.

12. *Juris-prudence,* Michael Doherty.
13. *Miracle At Philadelphia,* By Catherine Drinker Doen.
14. *The Least Dangerous Branch,* Alexander M. Bickel.
15. *Estranged Democracies,* Daniel Patrick Moynihan.
16. *British Constitutional Law,* Lord Templeman; Mich T. Mulan.
17. *Independent Counsel,* Charles A. Johnson.
18. *To Assure The Pride andd Confidence In The Electoral Process,* Jimmy Carter, Gerald Ford.
19. *Freedom of Information,* Patrick Birkin-Shaw.
20. *American Common Wealth,* James Bryce.
21. *Privacy and Press Freedom,* Raymond Wacks.
22. *Human Rights In The World,* A.H. Robertson, J.G. Merrils.
23. *Basic Documents On Human Rights,* Ian Browntic Q.C.
24. *The Warren Court,* Bernard Schwartz.
25. *The Supreme Court,* L. Baum.
26. *Story of the Constitution,* Richard Lee.
27. *Auto-Biography of Richard Nixon,* Richard Nixon.
28. *My White House Years,* Henry Kissinger.
29. *The Right And The Power,* Leon Jawaroski.
30. *To Set the Record Straight,* John J. Sirica.
31. *The Ends of Power,* H.R. Haldeman.
32. *Will,* Gordon Liddy.
33. *All the President's Men,* Woodward and Bernstein.
34. *The Final Days,* Woodward and Bernstein.

35. *Born Again,* Charlas A. Colson.

36. *Breach of Faith,* Theodore H. White.

37. *At That Point of Time,* Fred D. Thompson.

38. *John Marshall And The Compaign Of History,* Max Lenner.

39. *The Federalist Papers,* Hamilton, Madison and John Jay.

40. *The World of Richard Nixon,* O.L. Sulzeberger.

41. *The Warren Court,* Bernard Schwartz.

42. *The Whole Truth-The Watergate conspiracy,* Sam J. Ervin.

43. *The Whole Truth-The Watergate Consipracy,* Howard B. Lee.

44. *Chief Justice John Marshell,* H.O. Bishop.

45. *Constitution of India,* H.M. Seervai.

46. *The Law Of The Constitution,* A.V. Dicey.

47. *The Nature Of The Judicial Process,* Benjamin Woodward.

48. *The History of Second World War,* Sir Liewellyn Woodward.

49. *Democracy in America* Alexis De Tocquiville.

50. *The Days The Press Stopped,* David Rudestene.

51. *Presidential Impeachment,* John R. Labovitz.

52. *The Black-stone Commentaries on the Laws of England,* William Blackstone.

53. *Impeachment-The Constitutional Problems,* Raol Berger.

54. *The Prosecutors,* James B. Sterwart.

55. *The Turf Wars,* Daniel C. King.

56. *Legal Reform in Occupied Japan,* Alfred Oppler.

57. *The Himalayan Blunder,* Brig: J.P. Dalvi

58. *Germany,* Malcolom Pasley.

59. *The Tragedy of the Chinese Revolution (1925-27),* Harold J. Issacs.

60. *International Organisations,* A Le Roy Bernet.

61. *Working a Democratic Constitution,* Granwille Austin.

62. *A History of Political Theory,* Sabine & Thonson.

63. *John Foster Dulles,* Richard F. Immerman.

64. *United Nations-Divided World,* Adam Robert, Benedict.

65. *Administrative Law,* De Smith.

66. *Penorama of Indian Diplomacy,* N.M. Khilnani.

67. *Judicial Control of Administrative Action,* M.A. Fazl.

68. *Guilty,* Harold J. Rathox.

Index

Y